American Abolitionists

We work with leading authors to develop the
strongest educational materials in history,
bringing cutting-edge thinking and best learning
practice to a global market.

Under a range of well-known imprints, including
Longman, we craft high-quality print and electronic
publications which help readers to understand and
apply their content, whether studying or at work.

To find out more about the complete range of our
publishing please visit us on the World Wide Web at:
www.pearsoneduc.com

SEMINAR STUDIES IN HISTORY

American Abolitionists

STANLEY HARROLD

Longman

An imprint of **Pearson Education**

Harlow, England · London · New York · Reading, Massachusetts · San Francisco · Toronto · Don Mills, Ontario · Sydney
Tokyo · Singapore · Hong Kong · Seoul · Taipei · Cape Town · Madrid · Mexico City · Amsterdam · Munich · Paris · Milan

Pearson Education Limited
Edinburgh Gate
Harlow
Essex CM20 2JE
England
and Associated Companies throughout the world.

Visit us on the World Wide Web at:
www.pearsoneduc.com

First published 2001

ISBN 0-582-35738-1 PPR

British Library Cataloguing-in-Publication Data
A catalogue record for this book is
available from the British Library

Library of Congress Cataloging-in-Publication Data
Harrold, Stanley
   American abolitionists / Stanley Harrold.
      p. cm. -- (Seminar studies in history)
   Includes bibliographical references (p.) and index.
   ISBN 0-582-35738-1 (ppr)
      1. Abolitionists--United States--History. 2. Antislavery movements--United
States--History. I. Title. II. Series.

E449 .H298 2000
326´.8´0973--dc21   00-061472

Set by 7 in 10/12 Sabon Roman
Printed in Malaysia

For Lee Harrison Harrold

CONTENTS

INTRODUCTION TO THE SERIES

Such is the pace of historical enquiry in the modern world that there is an ever-widening gap between the specialist article or monograph, incorporating the results of current research, and general surveys, which inevitably become out of date. *Seminar Studies in History* is designed to bridge this gap. The series was founded by Patrick Richardson in 1966 and his aim was to cover major themes in British, European and world history. Between 1980 and 1996 Roger Lockyer continued his work, before handing the editorship over to Clive Emsley and Gordon Martel. Clive Emsley is Professor of History at the Open University, while Gordon Martel is Professor of International History at the University of Northern British Columbia, Canada, and Senior Research Fellow at De Montfort University.

All the books are written by experts in their field who are not only familiar with the latest research but have often contributed to it. They are frequently revised, in order to take account of new information and interpretations. They provide a selection of documents to illustrate major themes and provoke discussion, and also a guide to further reading. The aim of *Seminar Studies in History* is to clarify complex issues without over-simplifying them, and to stimulate readers into deepening their knowledge and understanding of major themes and topics.

NOTE ON REFERENCING SYSTEM

Readers should note that numbers in square brackets [5] refer them to the corresponding entry in the Bibliography at the end of the book (specific page numbers are given in italics). A number in square brackets preceded by *Doc.* [*Doc. 5*] refers readers to the corresponding item in the Documents section which follows the main text.

LIST OF ABBREVIATIONS

AAS	American Abolition Society
AASS	American Anti-Slavery Society
ACS	American Colonization Society
AFASS	American and Foreign Anti-Slavery Society
AMA	American Missionary Association
MASS	Massachusetts Anti-Slavery Society
NEASS	New England Anti-Slavery Society
PFASS	Philadelphia Female Anti-Slavery Society

PUBLISHER'S ACKNOWLEDGEMENTS

We are grateful to the following for permission to reproduce copyright material:

Plate 1, portrait of Elizabeth 'Mumbet' Freeman by Susan Anne Livingston Ridley Sedgwick, reproduced courtesy of the Massachusetts Historical Society; Plate 2, mob attacking the warehouse in Alton, Illinois © CORBIS, Plate 4, Frederick Douglass © Bettmann/CORBIS, Plate 7, Sojourner Truth © Bettmann/CORBIS, Plate 8 Gerrit Smith © CORBIS, all reproduced courtesy of Corbis; Plate 5, portrait of Lydia Maria Child, reproduced courtesy of The Schlesinger Library, Radcliffe Institute, Havard University.

While every effort has been made to trace the owners of copyright material, in a few cases this has proved impossible and we take this opportunity to offer our apologies to any copyright holders whose rights we have unwittingly infringed.

AUTHOR'S ACKNOWLEDGEMENTS

Although the author is responsible for all errors in fact and interpretation, this book has benefited from the work of many historians as well as the dedicated staff at Pearson Education. Special thanks are due to a half-dozen scholars who generously donated their expert advice. They are: Frederick J. Blue, Edmund L. Drago, Douglas R. Egerton, Sylvia Hoffert, John R. McKivigan, and Shirley J. Yee. Just as important was the wise counsel provided by the *Seminar Studies in History* Series Editor Gordon Martel and Pearson Education Senior Acquisitions Editor Emma Mitchell. Thanks are due as well to Heather McCallum, Sarah Bury and Verina Pettigrew for their efforts in preparing the book for publication.

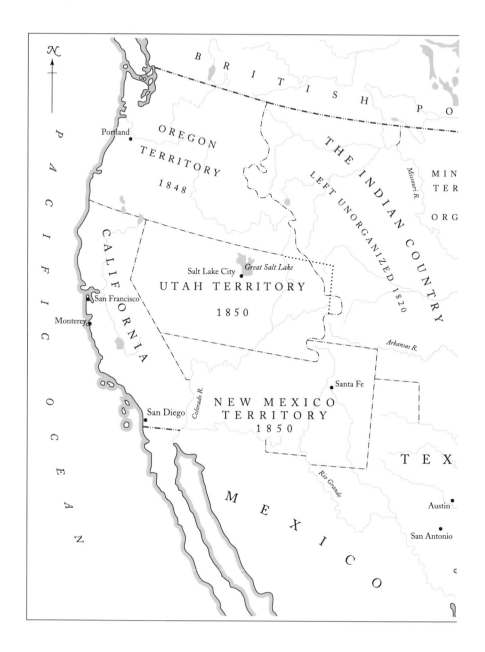

Map 1   The United States in September 1850

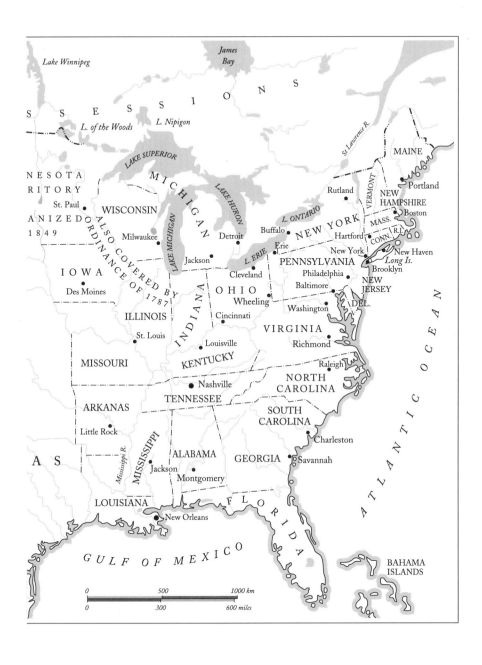

Lake Winnipeg

James
Bay

S   S   E   S   S   I   O   N   S

S

L. of the Woods   L. Nipigon

St Lawrence R.

MAINE

LAKE SUPERIOR

MICHIGAN

Rutland

VERMONT

Portland

NESOTA
RITORY

NEW
HAMPSHIRE

St. Paul

WISCONSIN

LAKE HURON

Boston

MASS.

ANIZED
1849

Milwaukee

LAKE MICHIGAN

Detroit

L. ONTARIO

Buffalo

NEW YORK

Hartford

CONN. R.I.

ALSO COVERED BY ORDINANCE OF 1787

Jackson

L. ERIE

Erie

New York

New Haven
Long Is.

IOWA

Cleveland

PENNSYLVANIA

Philadelphia

Brooklyn

NEW
JERSEY

Des Moines

OHIO

Baltimore

Wheeling

DEL.

ILLINOIS

Cincinnati

Washington

St. Louis

Louisville

INDIANA

VIRGINIA

Richmond

ATLANTIC OCEAN

MISSOURI

KENTUCKY

Raleigh

Nashville

NORTH
CAROLINA

ARKANAS

TENNESSEE

SOUTH
CAROLINA

Little Rock

Mississippi R.

MISSISSIPPI

Charleston

A   S

ALABAMA

GEORGIA

Savannah

Jackson

Montgomery

LOUISIANA

F L O R I D A

New Orleans

GULF   OF   MEXICO

BAHAMA
ISLANDS

0   500   1000 km

0   300   600 miles

PART ONE   INTRODUCTION

CHAPTER ONE

THE ABOLITIONISTS IN AMERICAN HISTORY

American abolitionists were people – black and white, female and male – who during the eighteenth and nineteenth centuries sought to end slavery and secure racial justice. They were part of a broader struggle within the Atlantic World against the enslavement of Africans and people of African descent. As a result of this struggle, a system of unfree labor that in 1750 existed throughout the British, Dutch, French, Portuguese, and Spanish empires in the New World had disappeared by 1888.

In the United States, which declared its independence from Great Britain in 1776, the antislavery effort faced especially determined opposition. Years of conflict between antislavery forces, located mainly in the North, and pro-slavery forces, centered in the South, preceded the emancipation of all American slaves. The unwillingness of African Americans to remain in bondage, profound economic and ideological change associated with the industrial revolution, and major evangelical revivals shaped a powerful antislavery impulse. But strong economic, cultural, and racial interests made American slavery a resilient phenomenon. Even after the formal abolition of slavery in 1865, these interests prevented African Americans from enjoying the same legal rights and economic opportunities as white Americans [59, 60, 91].

Nevertheless, abolitionism is one of the great reform movements in American history. It rivals the struggles for prohibition, women's rights, labor organization, and black civil rights in terms of longevity and impact. Like other reformers, abolitionists were controversial during their time and have remained so ever since. They were self-righteous, suspicious of compromise, often harsh in their language, capable of violence, and prone to factionalism.

The abolitionists' opposition to slavery led them to demand fundamental change in America's racial, economic, social, and political structure. Some of them espoused Christian anarchy and denounced the United States Constitution as proslavery, others insisted that the Constitution must be interpreted so as to abolish slavery. They challenged prevailing concepts of masculinity, while insisting that black men were as capable as white in such traditional masculine endeavors as fighting, wage-earning, and politics. The abolitionists' encouragement of women to participate in antislavery organizations led some of them to become feminists in a society that had long denied women a role in the public arena.

This book provides a brief but comprehensive history of these contentious, dedicated, often inconsistent, and intensely interesting reformers. Like other books in the *Seminar Studies in History* series, it reflects recent scholarly interpretations, while striving to maintain an accessible narrative. The emphasis is on the biracial character of the abolitionist movement, the impact of slaves on its development, and the increasingly aggressive tactics employed by abolitionists against slavery in the South. Subsidiary themes include the ties between abolitionism and women's rights, the interaction between peaceful and violent reform tactics, and the relationship between abolitionism and the coming of the Civil War.

WHO WERE THE ABOLITIONISTS?

When historian Betty Fladeland asked this question in 1964 she was concerned with the psychological orientation of those abolitionists active between 1830 and 1865 [208]. But the question of abolitionist identity has wider significance. Prior to the 1960s historians did not adequately differentiate between those who, during the antebellum decades, were *abolitionists* and those northern politicians and journalists who merely wanted to prevent the *extension* of slavery. This made it difficult to understand who the abolitionists were and what they stood for. The abolitionists, of course, had been aware of the differences between themselves and *nonextensionists*. But they also disagreed among themselves over what the proper definition of *abolitionist* should be.

In response to these difficulties, historians developed a precise characterization of abolitionists as individuals who, on the basis of moral principle, advocated *immediate* emancipation of the slaves and equal rights for African Americans without colonizing them beyond the borders of the United States. Active membership in antislavery societies, religious denominations, and radical political organizations pledged to these goals has become the chief means of identifying such people [102].

This precise distinction between immediate abolitionists and other antislavery groups, such as nonextentionists and those who urged the colonization of former slaves, has been extremely helpful in understanding abolitionism as it existed prior to the Civil War. But this definition's narrowness makes it misleading in several respects. It excludes those who sought gradually to abolish slavery and promote racial justice prior to the rise of immediatism during the late 1820s. It also excludes those antislavery politicians who – despite their strong abolitionist connections – were bound to honor conventional interpretations of the United States Constitution that recognized slavery as a legal institution under state control. Most important, as historian Douglas R. Egerton has recently pointed out, it excludes slave rebels and other black southerners who were practical abolitionists [126]. Therefore this book defines *abolitionism* more broadly. In stressing the biracial and intersectional character of abolitionism, it relies heavily on Egerton's insight and Merton L. Dillon's 1990 book *Slavery Attacked*, which portrays a growing alliance between southern slaves and northern abolitionists [66].

CHANGING INTERPRETATIONS

Few groups have been more intensely studied than the immediate abolitionists of the 1830s and 1840s. Historians have approached them in a variety of ways, and as twentieth-century events altered perspectives, differing interpretations of their motivation, character, and impact emerged. Over the years paradigms have shifted and new insights have contradicted older ones. Each layer of interpretation has contributed to a more sophisticated understanding of the movement.

In their memoirs and historical writings, former immediatists distinguished themselves from the gradual abolitionists who preceded them, described themselves as committed Christians, and maintained that they were the catalyst for the sectional struggle that led to general emancipation in 1865. The nationally oriented American historians of the late-nineteenth and early-twentieth centuries agreed. The abolitionists, in their estimation, were moral heroes who brought about the termination of human bondage in the United States [205].

Between the 1920s and the 1960s this image changed dramatically as 'revisionist' historians described immediate abolitionists more negatively [209 p. 4]. Several factors caused this reversal, but especially important was Ulrich B. Phillips's revival of the antebellum southern portrayal of slavery as a benevolent institution gradually civilizing people of African descent. Phillips suggested that white southerners would have peacefully ended slavery during the course of the nineteenth century had not abolitionists forced emancipation on them during the Civil War [102]. Rather than heroes, the abolitionists in this perspective were fanatics who pushed the country into a needless war.

This interpretation remained dominant into the 1950s as historians who emphasized agreement rather than conflict in American history argued that the Civil War was an avoidable tragedy. Avery O. Craven, James G. Randall, and others contended that northern abolitionists and their political allies raised irrational fears that undermined a bisectional agreement that would have allowed white southerners to deal on their own with the problem of slavery [147]. If, as Phillips argued, black people were content in slavery and paternalistic masters rarely mistreated them, why did abolitionists after 1830 insist that the institution be immediately abolished at the risk of sectional discord? If it were not the evil of slavery that motivated abolitionists, what led them to make such strident demands[205]?

For decades historians searched for answers to these questions. The search produced many insightful studies of northern social, economic, cultural, and psychological forces involved in shaping the immediatists. Of especial significance is Gilbert H. Barnes's 1933 portrayal of the role of evangelical revivalism in the North during the early decades of the nineteenth century [42]. John L. Thomas's 1963 attribution of the abolitionist impulse to New England culture and its westward expansion has also been extremely influential [177]. More directly in line with the revisionists was David Donald's dismissal in 1955 of the abolitionists as a displaced and neurotic New England social elite. According to Donald, these Yankees exploited the slavery issue merely to re-establish 'the traditional values of their class at home' or to assuage irrational feelings of guilt [67 *p. 36*].

During the 1960s, the Civil Rights movement encouraged a resurgence in positive assessments of the abolitionists. Supporting this tendency was Kenneth M. Stampp's *The Peculiar Institution*, published in 1956, which successfully challenged Phillips's portrayal of slavery as a benevolent institution and instead stressed its brutality [169]. 'Neo-abolitionist' historians began portraying abolitionists as psychologically healthy, middle-class liberals, who pioneered the struggle for black equality [116 *p. 236*]. Rather than constituting a displaced social elite, it now appeared that the abolitionists represented a rising northern entrepreneurial class, embodying modernizing values associated with industrialization. Their commitment to wage labor, social mobility, individualism, and education clearly conflicted with the traditional values associated with the South's rural culture and slave-labor economy [146, 169, 205].

Since the 1960s few historians have persisted in portraying the abolitionists as irresponsible fanatics fomenting a needless war over slavery. Instead, historians have focused on the degree of commitment among white abolitionists to racial justice, the respective roles of radicalism and conservatism in the movement, and the relevance of abolitionism to the sectional conflict that led to the Civil War. In pathbreaking articles and books published during the 1960s and 1970s, Leon F. Litwack and Jane H. Pease and William H. Pease contend that white abolitionists were unable to overcome the racial prejudices of their time. As a result they alienated black abolitionists and undermined their own efforts [221, 226, 144]. This view remains an important part of our understanding of the antislavery movement.

The issue of the abolitionists' identity as either conservative reformers or radicals is equally controversial. It has shaped historians' interpretations of the entire movement and their assessments of its impact. Barnes maintained that the moral absolutism and harsh rhetoric of social radicals such as William Lloyd Garrison and his New England associates destroyed their effectiveness. He contended that a larger and more moderate group of evangelical or church-oriented abolitionists led by Theodore D. Weld and Arthur and Lewis Tappan was more representative of the movement and more successful in spreading antislavery sentiment. In contrast, during the late 1960s, Aileen S. Kraditor and James Brewer Stewart maintained that it was the Garrisonians' radical critique of American society and their sophisticated methods of agitation that shaped abolitionism and accounted for its influence [115, 229].

The most important tendency in abolitionist studies during the period lasting from the 1960s through much of the 1980s, however, was to disengage the abolitionists from the sectional conflict over slavery. In 1961, Larry Gara argued persuasively that pervasive white abolitionist involvement in underground railroad efforts to help slaves reach freedom in the North and Canada was a deliberately fabricated myth. During the 1970s Merton L. Dillon and James Brewer Stewart wrote brilliant comprehensive studies, which documented the growing influence of abolitionism while concluding that the movement did not lead directly to emancipation [88, 65, 176].

Others went further, describing abolitionism solely in terms of northern culture in which the South and slavery had only symbolic value. Increasingly, studies of the abolitionists turned inward, seeking to understand what it meant to be part of the movement rather than how the movement affected broader events. Scholars described abolitionism as a surrogate religion, as part of community development, as a movement that used southerners as a negative reference group in a campaign for social control in the North. Increasingly it seemed abolitionists were simply seeking to absolve themselves from a morally corrupting proslavery culture rather than to force that culture to change [218, 231].

In historical literature abolitionists had gone from being charged with fomenting a needless war to being irrelevant. 'Sectional conflict, Civil War, and legal emancipation would probably have occurred even if there had been no active abolition movement,' wrote Lawrence J. Friedman in 1981 [210 *p. 194*].

NEW DIRECTIONS

During the 1990s historians' views of the abolitionists once again began to change. There was new interest in the relationship between the abolitionists and the slaves, in cooperation between black and white abolitionists, in abolitionism during the era of the American Revolution, and in the underground railroad. In addition, awareness of the role of gender in American culture produced a considerable amount of work not only on abolitionism and feminism, but on abolitionist concepts of masculinity.

This book follows recent work by Dillon, Herbert Aptheker, James L. Huston, and John Ashworth in emphasizing the role of slaves in shaping northern abolitionism. Black resistance to slavery not only amounted to practical abolitionism, it inspired antislavery sentiment in the North, and made the southern white reaction to abolitionism more desperate than it would have been otherwise. By recognizing the role of slave rebels and the growing willingness of antislavery northerners to intervene in the upper South, this book portrays abolitionism as an increasingly aggressive movement that helped push the South toward secession and the nation toward civil war [66, 39, 218, 41].

The interaction of black and white abolitionists in the North dates to the eighteenth century and grew closer as the nineteenth century progressed. While historians have long noted this interaction, it was Herbert Aptheker's 1941 article 'The Negro in the Abolitionist Movement' that first systematically investigated the role of black abolitionists [200]. Since then historians have given various degrees of prominence to African Americans within the northern movement. Of particular importance was the extended treatment they received in Benjamin Quarles's *The Black Abolitionists*, which was published in 1969. Quarles emphasized the biracial character of abolitionism while recognizing that racial bias among white abolitionists had a negative impact on the movement [149].

Since 1969 three more general book-length studies of black abolitionists have been published [46, 144, 195]. There have also been numerous biographies of black antislavery leaders, most of which emphasize the differences between them and their white colleagues. There was, however, a tendency during the 1990s to stress the ability of black and white abolitionists to cooperate in challenging the racial *status quo* of their time [40, 62, 96, 224]. This book reflects these recent studies, especially in regard to such physical efforts as the underground railroad and opposition to the enforcement of the fugitive slave laws.

There have also been numerous studies during the past three decades dealing with abolitionist notions of gender. Several such studies focus on the abolitionists in order to understand broader nineteenth-century American perceptions of femininity and masculinity. The abolitionists' understandings of gender are also important in their own right in regard to the emergence of the women's rights movement and in exploring conflicted abolitionist views regarding peaceful and violent means. It was in the context of abolitionism during the 1830s that northern women first challenged patriarchy. Meanwhile a new feminized masculinity encouraged abolitionists to endorse nonviolence while traditional concepts of manhood led them to praise those who took up arms against slavery [126]. Several historians contend that it was not until the sectional conflict itself became violent during the 1850s that abolitionists embraced violent means [185, 203, 225]. But this study indicates that violence played a role in the movement from its beginnings.

In all, abolitionism was a radical movement shaped by the refusal of African Americans to accept enslavement. Although the abolitionists did not by themselves bring about the Civil War and emancipation, their efforts to shape opinion and their aggressive actions had an important impact. Although the abolitionists failed to bring about racial justice, and white abolitionists were not fully conscious of their own racism, the movement pushed a reluctant nation toward egalitarian goals.

PART TWO   ANALYSIS

CHAPTER TWO

EARLY ABOLITIONISM

Africans and African Americans sought to free themselves as soon as slavery came into existence in the British North American colonies during the seventeenth century. By the end of that century a few white Puritans and Quakers in New England and the middle colonies had begun to express reservations concerning the morality of employing slave labor. But it was not until the latter half of the eighteenth century that religious, economic, and ideological change produced authentic abolitionist movements among black and white Americans. These early abolitionists – both slave and free – had considerable success in the North, some in the upper South, and only a negative impact in the deep South.

Before discussing their successes and failures, their motivations, and their impact, however, it is necessary to consider briefly the character of the institution against which they contended.

AMERICAN SLAVERY

Slavery in a wide variety of forms had existed throughout the world since ancient times. In the Greek and Roman civilizations slaves served as soldiers, teachers, domestic servants, concubines, and wives, as well as agricultural workers. Slaves might be people of any race who lost their freedom as a result of war or religious persecution. Although custom varied according to place and time, slaves in the ancient world did not always serve for life, their children did not necessarily inherit their condition, and they did not lose all their customary rights. Sometimes slaves rose to positions of authority, owned property, and were able to pass that property on to their children.

Slavery declined in Europe during the Middle Ages as serfdom became the principal form of unfree labor on that continent. But bondage continued to thrive in Africa and the Near East. For centuries thousands of black people from south of the Sahara Desert served as slaves in the Islamic world. Many others were enslaved in sub-Saharan Africa. By the fifteenth century, wars fought as part of a process of state formation constituted the principal cause of enslavement in West Africa, where most of the people who became American slaves originated [134].

Being a slave in West Africa could be a harrowing experience. This was especially the case for the first generation of an enslaved people. But as succeeding generations of slaves became acculturated they gained customary rights, formed families, and gained a right to the land they farmed. It was when West-African warfare conjoined with European expansion during the fifteenth century that a new more brutal and potentially dehumanizing form of slavery came into existence. In order to provide laborers for their colonies in the Americas, European nations created the Atlantic slave trade. As a result of this barbaric trade between Africa and the Americas, millions of Africans and their African-American descendants experienced this new type of slavery.

While there were important similarities between Old World forms of slavery and slavery in the Americas, it is the differences that are most significant. With the emergence of Brazil and the Caribbean islands during the early 1500s as producers of sugar, a system of enslavement based on race came into existence. Although there were significant numbers of American-Indian slaves, usually white Europeans enslaved black Africans. The great majority of these slaves lost their customary rights and engaged in unskilled agricultural labor on large plantations [45, 114].

This form of *chattel slavery*, in which humans are legally reduced to the status of livestock, existed in an extreme form in the British North American colonies that later became the United States. In Latin America, where few Europeans settled, Africans were needed to fill positions that opened routes to freedom. They became artisans and militiamen as well as concubines and wives. They rapidly assimilated to the prevailing European culture and converted to Christianity as a result of active Roman Catholic missionary efforts. In British North America, however, where there was a large population of European descent and black people were not needed as free workers and mates, routes to freedom were more rare and whites resisted acculturation among blacks [139].

The most fully documented accounts indicate that the first Africans in the British North American colonies arrived in 1619 at Jamestown, Virginia aboard a Dutch warship. Shortly after their arrival these twenty men and women were sold not as slaves but as indentured servants. This meant that, like the majority of Europeans who arrived in the British colonies during the seventeenth century, they lost their freedom and labored for a master for a term of years. It was not until the middle decades of the century that masters in Virginia and neighboring Maryland began to contend that Africans, unlike Europeans, must serve for life [114].

During the next forty years the rising price of white indentured servants, combined with growing British control over the Atlantic slave trade, made black slavery the predominant form of labor in Virginia, Maryland, and the other British colonies to their south. Whites determined not only that blacks would serve for life, but that slave status passed from mother to child, and that *all* black people must be assumed to be slaves unless they could prove otherwise. Enslaved Africans and their descendants lost their ability to testify against whites in court, to own property, to engage in business, to vote, to marry legally, and to move about freely. In the British colonies to the north of Virginia and Maryland, black slavery never became the dominant form of labor. Slaves in the North generally enjoyed better prospects. Even so, the northern and southern slave systems were similar until the end of the eighteenth century when northern states began to abolish human bondage [127].

By 1790, when the total American population was about four million, there were nearly 700,000 slaves in the United States, with all but 40,000 living in the South. By 1830 the enslaved population had risen to two million within a total population of 12,500,000 and all but 3,500 of the slaves were in the South. By 1860, when the country's total population was just over thirty million, nearly all of the four million slaves lived in the southern states stretching from the Atlantic coast to Texas.

Although the typical slaveholder owned few slaves, the typical slave labored on a large planation. Depending upon region and climate, slaves planted, cultivated, and harvested such staple crops as tobacco, cotton, rice, hemp, or sugar. By the early nineteenth century, slaves in the Chesapeake region of Virginia and Maryland were cultivating wheat, corn, and vegetables. At various locations in the South smaller numbers of slaves engaged in lumbering, manufacturing, and mining. In urban areas slaves served as artisans, day laborers, and as domestic servants. The employment of enslaved black women ranged from field work to domestic service and child care.

The labor provided by slaves propelled the southern economy and created a small but powerful master class that dominated the region economically and politically from the late seventeenth century through the Civil War. From early in the colonial era, a slaveholding gentry, composed of interrelated families, governed as county magistrates and provincial legislators. Later, slaveholders dominated southern state governments. They made law, appealed to racial solidarity in order to gain the support of less well-to-do whites, and shaped a masculine code of honor that subordinated individual liberty to the protection of community interests [90, 192].

Slaveholders, such as George Washington, Thomas Jefferson, and James Madison, led the United States in its war for independence. In 1787 they drafted a national constitution that provided implicit protection for slavery. Between 1789 and 1850 all but three of the men who served as president of the United States were members of this class. Slaveholders constituted a powerful bloc in Congress, controlled the Democratic party from its founding in 1828, and dominated the Supreme Court [78].

Just as important, southern staple crops produced by slave labor had an essential role in the American economy. Cotton was the country's principal product during the nineteenth century and by far its most lucrative export. Therefore slaveholders exercised economic power in the North. Not only did they supply the textile industry of New England with its raw material, they purchased much of the grain, beef, and pork produced in the states of the Old Northwest. Slaveholders also benefited from the racism of white northerners, who generally shared a low estimation of African Americans and had little inclination to interfere with slavery [120].

AFRICANS, AFRICAN AMERICANS, AND QUAKERS

As soon as slavery came into existence in America, its victims sought freedom through self-purchase, court action, and escape. More rarely, but with far greater dramatic and psychological impact, they sought freedom through revolt. In 1676 at least eighty black men fought on the side of white rebel Nathaniel Bacon in a failed attempt to overthrow the authority of Virginia's slaveholding landed gentry. In New York City in 1712 about thirty-five enslaved Africans, with a few white and American-Indian allies, arose against their masters, burned several buildings, and killed nine men who attempted to douse the fires. At Stono Bridge, South Carolina in 1739 about one hundred slaves seized arms and ammunition and began marching south toward Spanish Florida, where authorities promised freedom to slaves who escaped from the British colonies [66, 91, 104].

White authorities crushed these rebellions and others as well. In each instance the failed black insurrectionists and their white and Indian abettors faced brutal punishments. In the New York case, for example, those convicted were variously hanged, burned at the stake, starved to death, or broken on the wheel [104]. Yet, as Carl Degler, Eugene Genovese, and other historians note, such rebellions aimed at escape from rather than abolition of slavery. Motivated by African and Christian religious beliefs, African rebels sought to establish autonomous communities and – if successful – might themselves become slaveholders [91]. The early slave rebellions, nevertheless, helped convince some white Americans that it was better gradually to abolish slavery than perpetually to experience such uprisings.

Chief among such antislavery whites during the colonial era were members of the Society of Friends, commonly known as Quakers. As religious dissenters, the ancestors of these pietistic Protestants had endured persecution in England before seeking refuge in America. They settled in New Jersey during the 1670s and in 1681 William Penn established the

Quaker colony of Pennsylvania. Quakers also settled in all of the other British colonies in North America and many of them became slaveholders. But the Society of Friends' radical doctrine that God's inner light united all humans and the sect's commitment to nonviolence led a few Quakers to be sensitive to the brutal nature of slavery and its potential for sparking interracial warfare [36, 79]. Like later abolitionists, they assumed that God might use such violence to punish a society for keeping an unwilling people in bondage [*Doc. 1*].

As early as 1693, Philadelphia Quaker leader George Keith published *An Exhortation and Caution to Friends Concerning Buying and Keeping of Negroes*. During the 1730s Benjamin Lay, who had owned slaves on the West Indian island of Barbados and later moved to Pennsylvania, labored to convince Quakers of the sinfulness of the practice. Lay and other abolitionists of his generation faced considerable resistance within the Society of Friends. They found it easier to persuade other Quakers to stop buying and selling slaves than to make the financial sacrifice entailed in freeing them.

Nevertheless, from the 1740s through the 1760s, Quaker abolitionists John Woolman and Anthony Benezet convinced most Quakers to cease all connection with slavery. Woolman traveled constantly in his native New Jersey as well as in Pennsylvania, New England, Maryland, and Virginia in order to address his antislavery arguments to Quaker meetings. He contended that slaveholding was incompatible with Christian morality and that all human beings had a right to freedom. Although Benezet stayed closer to his Philadelphia home, his essays had a wide impact in both America and Great Britain [68, 79, 168].

In 1758 Woolman and Benezet gained control of the crucial Philadelphia Meeting, condemned slaveholders and slave traders, and excluded them from positions of leadership. Other Quaker meetings followed this example. In Maryland in 1768, in New England in 1770, and in New York in 1774 they ended Quaker participation in the slave trade. During the American War for Independence Quakers in the North freed their slaves and by 1788 those in Maryland and Virginia had done so as well.

But, as these achievements suggest, prior to the American Revolution and for years thereafter, antislavery Quakers were – like early slave rebels – abolitionists only to a limited degree. Black insurrectionists sought mainly to free themselves from bondage, and Quakers, such as Lay, Woolman, and Benezet, sought mainly to free other Quakers from the sin of slaveholding [168]. Quakers were also reluctant to admit black people to their meetings without arranging for segregated 'Negro benches' [68 *pp. 120–1*]. Even so, members of the Society of Friends were predominant among white abolitionists through the 1820s. After that decade Quakers remained active opponents of slavery in the upper South and continued to constitute an important segment of the northern antislavery movement.

ABOLITIONISM DURING THE REVOLUTIONARY ERA

It took major religious, economic, and ideological transformations during the mid- and late-eighteenth century to spread antislavery sentiment beyond the ranks of African Americans and Quakers and to establish an assumption that all persons should be free. Among the developments that changed human perspectives in regard to slavery were the spread of rationalism, commercialism, evangelicalism, and revolution.

Rationalism – a product of the European intellectual movement known as the Enlightenment – and commercialism – an economic expansion associated with the industrial revolution – created an Atlantic World in which, by the late 1700s, slavery seemed to be increasingly out of place. Both of these great developments emphasized order, predictability, efficiency, individualism, and education. Influenced by Renaissance humanism and the seventeenth-century physics of Isaac Newton, Enlightenment philosophers, such as John Locke, sought natural laws for an orderly human society. They attributed human differences to environmental factors and proposed that all human beings shared natural rights.

Simultaneously, merchant capitalists sought to rationalize business relationships, employ literate and efficient workers, and create a stable economy. From each of these perspectives slave labor systems that rested on force rather than reason, ignorance rather than education, and traditional rather than modern values appeared to be anachronistic [59].

In contrast to rationalism and commercialism, Protestant evangelicalism emphasized emotion. But evangelicalism was as important as the other two developments in shaping the course of American abolitionism. Widespread religious revivalism took place in the British colonies in North America during the early- and mid-eighteenth century. Known as the Great Awakening, this movement weakened church organization, de-emphasized ritual, and subordinated theology to enthusiasm. Revivalists, exemplified by George Whitefield, stressed that all who had faith in God could gain salvation regardless of their standing in society [53]. This suggested that all people without reference to wealth, education, or race, were valuable in God's eyes, and Whitefield and other revivalists often preached to racially integrated audiences.

The Great Awakening also encouraged voluntary action among converts as a means not only of demonstrating their own state of grace but of serving God's design. This led some whites to perceive that they had an obligation to help the downtrodden. Perhaps even more important, the Great Awakening led to the conversion of the great mass of African Americans to Christianity. Particularly in the North and the Chesapeake, conversion narrowed the cultural gap between black and white Americans. Consequently more whites – beyond the Society of Friends – were able to perceive blacks to be proper objects of Christian benevolence [73]. At the same time the way opened for blacks to develop a church-related institutional framework for antislavery activism [104].

It was the political and social upheaval associated with the American Revolution that catalyzed the forces of rationalism, commercialism, and evangelicalism on behalf of an abolitionist movement that transcended black rebels and the Society of Friends. When during the 1760s white Americans reacted against British policies that threatened their economic and political interests, they had difficulty denying the injustice imposed by slavery on African Americans. White revolutionaries asserted that the British monarchy sought to deprive them of their natural rights and reduce them to slaves. This raised the question of what they were doing to those they held in bondage. George Washington warned in 1774 that unless white Americans defended their natural rights they would become 'as tame and abject, as the blacks we rule over with such arbitrary sway' [80 *p. 322*]. Revolutionary propagandist Thomas Paine put it more pointedly in urging white Americans to contemplate 'with what consistency, or decency they complain so loudly of attempts to enslave them, while they hold so many hundred thousands in slavery; and annually enslave many thousands more' [189 *p. 3*].

These contradictions were just as obvious to the slaves themselves and African Americans took the lead in pressing for a broader abolitionist movement. As early as 1766 slaves in Charleston, South Carolina marched through the streets shouting, 'Liberty!' [66 *pp. 28–9*]. Slave escapes mounted in the southern colonies and to gain the freedom of themselves and their families black men fought on both sides during the American War for Independence [136].

Meanwhile self-consciously abolitionist African Americans prodded state courts and legislatures to act against slavery. Blacks had long resorted to the courts in both the North and South in search of freedom. But now, especially in the North, they began to emphasize a universal right to liberty rather than the individual claims to free ancestry and the legal technicalities that had characterized earlier freedom suits. During the early 1780s Elizabeth Freeman, Quok Walker, and other slaves initiated law suits that led to a Massachusetts supreme court decision declaring slavery to be 'effectively abolished' in that state [198 *p. 114*]. In Connecticut, Massachusetts, and New Hampshire African Americans organized during the 1770s to petition state legislatures for gradual abolition on the grounds that they 'in common with all other men [had] a natural and unalienable right to that freedom which the Great Parent of the Universe hath bestowed equally on all mankind' [22 *p. 23*].

Black men fought on the Patriot side at Lexington and Concord in April 1775 and at the Battle of Bunker Hill in June of that year. Later black men – and a few black women – served in the Continental Army and in northern state militia units during the long War for Independence. That service helped create public sentiment among northern whites that led not only Massachusetts, but also New Hampshire, and Vermont – which did not become a state until 1791 – to end slavery within their bounds during the 1780s. Black military service and petitioning campaigns encouraged other northern states to initiate policies of gradual abolition [148].

By the 1790s Richard Allen and Absalom Jones – both of whom were former slaves from Delaware – had established independent black churches in Philadelphia, beginning the process by which these black institutions became centers for abolitionist activities [137, *Doc. 3*]. But the leading black abolitionist of the Revolutionary era was Prince Hall of Boston. Beginning during the 1770s, he led petition efforts against slavery in Massachusetts, emphasized natural rights doctrines, sought state funds for black schools, worked to protect free blacks against attempts to kidnap them into slavery, and called for the abolition of the external slave trade [112].

It was also during the era of the American Revolution that white abolitionists organized the first antislavery societies. Quakers led in such efforts but were later joined by individuals chiefly motivated by rationalist precepts. For example, Quakers in Philadelphia formed in 1775 the first antislavery society in the world, but when the society reorganized in 1787 numerous non-Quakers joined. Among them were Benjamin Rush and Benjamin Franklin. In New York, Revolutionary leaders Alexander Hamilton and John Jay helped organize a similar society [83, 198].

Such individuals believed the existence of slavery contradicted the values of America's republican revolution, but they also acted out of fear of divine punishment. By the 1790s antislavery societies, dominated by Quakers, had spread as far south as Virginia. Although these southern antislavery societies were small, conservative, and ephemeral, they left a legacy of interracial cooperation against slavery that lasted to the eve of the Civil War [38, 207, 215].

The efforts of black and white abolitionists were instrumental in the decisions during the Revolutionary Era to end slavery in the northern states. They also played a role in convincing slaveholders in the Chesapeake to manumit individual slaves [44, 197]. Yet this early antislavery movement had several features that distinguish it from northern abolitionism during the antebellum years of the nineteenth century.

First, while the black and white abolitionists of the period had similar goals and cooperated, they never belonged to the same organizations. Secondly, the early abolitionists advocated *gradual* emancipation and such northern leaders as Rush, Jay, and Hamilton were reluctant to free their own black servants. Thirdly, white abolitionists of the era did not advocate equal rights for African Americans and racial justice was not a product of emancipation in the northern states [132].

Finally, during the late 1700s, abolitionists lacked a national perspective. A meeting held in Philadelphia in 1794 created the American Convention for Promoting the Abolition of Slavery and Improving the Condition of the African Race. This organization provided a forum for the various state and local antislavery societies [79], but the societies rarely dealt with slavery in areas beyond the borders of the states in which they existed. Once a northern state had abolished slavery or provided for its gradual abolition, most white abolitionists who resided within its bounds assumed that their work was done. They believed incorrectly that antislavery movements in the southern states would carry on where they left off [73].

REACTION AND REBELLION

In fact by the mid-1780s the Revolutionary antislavery impulse had peaked among white Americans and had begun a general decline. In 1785 the state legislatures in New York and New Jersey narrowly defeated plans for gradual abolition. It would be fourteen more years in New York and nineteen more in New Jersey before similar plans passed. In 1787 the Confederation Congress banned slavery in the Northwest Territory but that same year delegates at the Philadelphia Constitutional Convention produced a document – The United States Constitution – that provided important protection for the continued existence of slavery [78, 198].

Under this constitution slaveholders gained enhanced representation in Congress, a guarantee that the external slave trade would continue for another twenty years, and a mandate for a fugitive slave law that would enable masters to recover escaped slaves. In 1790 Congress retreated from an attempt to assert its authority over the domestic slave trade and slavery in the states [138]. During the following decade the pace of manumissions slowed in the Chesapeake and antislavery societies in that region began a long decline. As the cultivation of cotton spread in the deep South and prices for slaves rose, masters in Virginia, Maryland, and Delaware began to sell slaves south rather than free them. Narrowly focused as they were, northern abolitionists did little more than lament this turn of events [138, 207].

Several factors account for the failure of the Revolutionary generation to move more consistently for abolition. Chief among them were the greater dependence in the southern states on slave labor than existed in the North and a correspondingly greater reluctance among southern whites to create a large class of free blacks. The southern economy required slave labor and nearly all white southerners believed slavery had to be continued in order to control African Americans. But more complicated social and cultural forces unleashed by the American Revolution also exercised negative influences on antislavery sentiment.

Fear of egalitarian and democratic forces that had been unleashed by the Revolution played an important role. Southern planters, who worried that revolutionary ideology encouraged self-assertion among African Americans, grew increasingly convinced that perpetual slavery was the best means of quelling that spirit. Meanwhile, events in 1786 and 1789 led wealthy northerners to become increasingly conservative on economic and political issues. In the former year Daniel Shays led a rebellion of poor white farmers in western Massachusetts that seemed to threaten the social order. In the latter year the French Revolution unleashed a leveling ideology. As poor white northerners sought greater power, northern elites became more sympathetic to the southern masters' predicament and tended to make common cause with them [41, 179].

Simultaneously, as poor whites sought to improve their social standing during the Revolutionary Era, race replaced class as the major point of division in American society. In the South, slaveholders appealed to racial unity in a successful campaign to convince nonslaveholding whites to support slavery and black inferiority [85]. In the North, poorer whites, who during the colonial period shared a similar class interest with African Americans, increasingly interpreted social status in racial terms and sought to restrict black access to schools, churches, and employment [104].

An emerging consensus among whites maintained that African Americans were unsuited for freedom and citizenship. A new scientific racism, which rejected the Enlightenment's environmental explanation of racial differences, supported this assumption. By the 1780s Thomas Jefferson's contention that 'scientific observation' proved that blacks were inherently 'inferior to whites in the endowments of both body and mind' found few challengers outside the African-American community [26 *pp. 128–43*].

The idea that persons of African descent were naturally suited for enslavement and therefore content with their unfree status began its long career. Acting on this belief, Congress during the 1790s excluded persons of African ancestry from the benefits of citizenship in 'a white man's country' [190 *p. 167*]. In the Chesapeake, the advance of emancipation stalled because whites feared that free blacks would constitute a growing dependent, criminal, and revolutionary class [44]. It seemed that black people had no place in America except as slaves.

African Americans and their white allies refused to accept this view. A few white abolitionists in the North and the Chesapeake continued to cooperate with African Americans in bringing freedom suits to court and in helping free blacks illegally held in slavery. Though in decline, white abolition societies in the Chesapeake, backed by the American Convention, continued to petition state legislatures for gradual abolition [180, 79, 52]. In the North – and to a lesser extent in the Chesapeake – black abolitionists pressed on for emancipation and racial justice, while urging the newly free to strive for middle-class respectability in order to alleviate white fears [232]. More ominously for slaveholders, southern slaves clung to the egalitarian principles of the American Revolution. The French Revolution and the black revolution in Haiti, which began in 1791 under the leadership of Toussaint Louverture and ended successfully in 1804, encouraged them to do so [91, 126].

In fact, the war for black liberation in Haiti fundamentally influenced the course of American abolitionism. The ability of black Haitians to win freedom and independence on the battlefield against European troops belied pseudoscientific depictions of African Americans as members of a docile race who were content in slavery. Beginning during the 1790s, northern – and some southern – abolitionists applauded the Haitian struggle for liberty and warned that black Americans would follow the Haitian example if not emancipated [66]. By the early 1830s northern abolitionists had begun to compare Louverture to George Washington, to regard him as an archetypical black hero, and to suggest that he and others like him were agents of divine retribution [10(b), 199].

It was well before the 1830s, however, that pockets of black revolution materialized in the South. As the war in Haiti progressed, white planters left the island with their slaves seeking refuge in South Carolina, Virginia, and Louisiana. The Haitian slaves spread a commitment to violent abolitionism among local blacks, who were well aware of the United States' own revolutionary principles. While rumors of revolt plagued South Carolina's slaveholders, a major slave conspiracy formed in Virginia in 1800 and a large slave revolt occurred in Louisiana in 1811 [66].

Unlike earlier slave conspiracies and revolts among American slaves, the black rebels led by Gabriel in Virginia and by Charles Deslondes in Louisiana aimed at abolition rather than simply freeing themselves. They planned to attack centers of white authority – Richmond in Virginia and New Orleans in Louisiana – rather than to escape from that authority, and they endorsed principles of universal liberty [70, 126].

Gabriel's plan went awry when two of his associates betrayed it to white authorities and a raging thunderstorm prevented his followers from gathering at the appointed time. A force of seven hundred well-armed white men, which included United States Army regulars, overwhelmed Deslondes's band of nearly two hundred men and women. In each instance white authorities executed the rebel leaders and over twenty of their followers. But Gabriel and Deslondes left revolutionary networks among slaves and some sympathetic whites [70, 126]. Gabriel, who was far better known among his contemporaries than Deslondes, also became part of abolitionist lore as a brave slave rebel and as a symbol of African-American manhood [10(a)].

While the actions of both of these men increased southern white fear of race war and determination to be more vigilant against signs of slave unrest, it was Gabriel who had the larger impact on the broader struggle over slavery in the South. Following the exposure of his plot, the antiabolitionist reaction intensified. Antislavery societies in Delaware, Maryland, and Virginia – which had begun to decline during the 1790s – disbanded, became only sporadically active, or struggled on with diminishing memberships [44, 52].

Increasingly, these organizations and other forums for antislavery opinion among whites became receptive to the argument that emancipation must be linked with the expatriation of free blacks. Otherwise, it seemed, a growing free black class would become the chief abettor of slave revolt. For a time African-American leaders, perceiving the limits on black freedom in the United States, favored leaving America [133]. But, by the end of the second decade of the nineteenth century, most had changed their mind. Maturing black voluntary institutions, a new religious revival, a market revolution, the rise of slavery as a political issue between the North and the South, and the emergence of a new generation of black and white abolitionists would soon create a dynamic movement for emancipation and black rights in the United States.

CHAPTER THREE

THE RISE OF IMMEDIATISM

The proslavery reaction that began during the last decades of the eighteenth century lasted well into the nineteenth century. It provided the context for the more racially integrated, comprehensive, and aggressive northern antislavery movement that emerged during the late 1820s and early 1830s. As gradual abolition societies withered in a country increasingly polarized by race, a new generation of black and white abolitionists urged masters *immediately* to emancipate their slaves on the basis of Christian morality, self-interest, and national salvation.

Although this 'modern abolitionism' [4(b)] ran counter to mounting racism among white Americans and attracted only a small minority of activists, it spread rapidly across the North during the 1830s. Shortly after the middle of that decade, internal divisions appeared in the movement as immediatists disagreed among themselves over such issues as political action, the role of churches, and the participation of women. From the start, too, northern abolitionists were ambivalent concerning their commitment to peaceful means at a time when there were violent initiatives by southern black abolitionists and violent antiabolitionism in northern cities [87].

COLONIZATION

A precursor of immediate abolitionism was the movement to colonize black Americans in West Africa, Haiti, or in other locations beyond the borders of the United States. During the early 1800s, as their hope for racial justice in America declined, black abolitionists found the prospect of migration to a more hospitable land attractive [178]. Meanwhile the American Colonization Society (ACS) – established in Washington, DC in 1816 – introduced many whites, some of whom later became immediatists, to antislavery activism. But by the late 1820s the ACS had become the foil for those who desired a racially inclusive society in the United States [171].

As early as 1773 some African Americans in Massachusetts announced their intention upon gaining freedom 'to transport ourselves to some part of the Coast of Africa, where we propose settlement' [*Doc. 2*]. Much of this early black interest in emigration existed among those who had been born in Africa and hoped to return to the land of their birth. But, as Barbados-born Prince Hall demonstrated in 1787 when he and seventy others petitioned the Massachusetts legislature for transportation to Africa, interest in such ventures also resulted from diminished prospects in America [104, 138].

During the first two decades of the nineteenth century, the leading African-American proponent of African colonization was Paul Cuffe, a Quaker sea captain and entrepreneur from Westport, Massachusetts. Cuffe cooperated first with British abolitionists in transporting colonists from the United States to Great Britain's African colony for free blacks at Sierra Leone. Then, just prior to his death in 1817, he worked with the ACS in the establishment of its similar colony at nearby Liberia [178].

Cuffe enjoyed the support of such influential black abolitionists as Richard Allen and James Forten, both of whom resided in Philadelphia. This reflected a strain of black nationalism within the African-American community that persists to the present. During the 1850s, such prominent black abolitionists as Henry Highland Garnet and Martin R. Delany promoted emigration to Africa or Haiti as a means of improving the standing of people of color in the United States and the world. But, by the year of Cuffe's death, most African Americans regarded the United States as their native land and were suspicious of the ACS [104, 133].

That suspicion was well founded as the ACS represented a continuing white reaction against racial justice in the United States. Ostensibly, the organization had two goals. The first was to bring about the gradual abolition of slavery by using African colonization to reduce fear among whites that manumission would result in an ever increasing and dangerous free black population. The second was to employ black Americans as Christian missionaries in Africa [171]. Yet, because the ACS's efforts coincided with movements in the states of the upper South to expel free African Americans, there was considerable fear within the black community that the organization's real aim was to strengthen slavery through the forceful removal of all free black people from America [104].

BLACK ABOLITIONIST VIOLENCE

Some free African Americans, by quietly spreading antislavery ideas among slaves, encouraging slaves to escape, and harboring escapees, helped create a belief among white southerners that all free blacks were dangerous abolitionists [44]. However, the actions of violent black liberators in the South and the words of northern black advocates of forceful abolition had a more dramatic impact on popular opinion. Startling events in 1822, 1829, and 1831 intensified fear of slave revolt in the South and influenced the rise of immediatism in the North.

During the first of these years black informants revealed to white authorities what seemed to be plans for a slave uprising in Charleston, South Carolina. The leader of the conspiracy was Denmark Vesey, a free black man influenced by the American, French, and Haitian revolutions, evangelical Christianity, antislavery pamphlets, and African spiritualism. After the arrest and execution of Vesey and thirty-five others, Charleston and South Carolina put harsh restrictions on free blacks and enacted other measures designed to strengthen human bondage [71].

Until recently, historians have believed that Vesey's impact was confined to South Carolina. Thanks largely to the work of historian Peter Hinks, however, it is now clear that unrest within Charleston's black community – if not Vesey himself – had a direct impact on black abolitionist David Walker, who published his *Appeal to the Colored Citizens of the World* in Boston in 1829. Walker, who had been born free in North Carolina in 1796 or 1797, visited Charleston during the early 1820s and attended camp meetings conducted by the same African Methodist Episcopal (AME) church to which Vesey belonged. When he migrated to Boston in the mid-1820s, Walker carried with him a concept of black manhood and a willingness to advocate antislavery violence that influenced black and white northern abolitionists. Walker also convinced white southerners that a clandestine abolitionist network threatened the existence of slavery [103].

Walker's *Appeal* infused militancy into the northern antislavery movement. His portrayal of colonization as proslavery rather than antislavery was not new or exceptional among black abolitionists of his time but he added urgency. He asserted the right of African Americans to United States citizenship. He urged black men to redeem themselves from subserviency by defending their loved ones. 'Had you not rather be killed,' he asked, 'than be a slave to a tyrant, who takes the life of your mother, wife, and dear little children?' [17 *p. 89*]. Most significant of all, Walker recalled race warfare in Haiti and assured African Americans that God would raise up a black warrior to 'deliver you through him from your deplorable and wretched condition under the Christians of America' [*Doc. 4*].

Walker, who died of tuberculosis less than a year after the publication of his pamphlet, frightened southern whites by his ability to circulate his revolutionary document among free blacks and slaves in the port cities of the South. By relying on black and white seamen who sailed from Boston and on a black network in the South, Walker demonstrated that an alliance between northern abolitionists and southern slaves was possible [66]. Therefore when slave preacher Nat Turner led a slave uprising in Southampton County, Virginia in 1831, southern whites assumed that he was acting in conjunction with antislavery northerners, although no proof to that effect has every been found.

Even more than Walker, Turner shaped the context of American abolitionism during the nineteenth century. Although Turner acted at a time of slave unrest in Virginia, was aware of the Haitian revolution, and America's own revolutionary heritage, he was more religious visionary than political revolutionary. He believed, through a variety of portents, that God had chosen him to liberate his people through violence. When he and his band of sixty to seventy men killed fifty-seven white men, women, and children – the largest number of white Americans ever to die during a slave revolt – they raised southern fear of violent abolitionism to an unprecedented level [140].

In the short run, it seemed that Turner had only a negative impact on the antislavery movement. After being overwhelmed by white militia, he and seventeen of his associates were hanged. In nearby portions of Virginia and North Carolina, whites killed at least one hundred other African Americans whom they suspected of sharing Turner's commitment to revolt. In the North, both black and white abolitionists recoiled at the bloodshed Turner had unleashed. Yet there were few abolitionists of either race who did not respect him. They compared him to Louverture, to Gabriel, to George Washington, and to other liberators. In particular, they warned southern whites that without immediate abolition other slaves would follow Turner's example in violently challenging slaveholders [102].

THE MARKET REVOLUTION AND EVANGELICALISM

It is unlikely that a single white American of the antebellum era fully overcame racial bias against African Americans. But a variety of economic and cultural phenomena, combined with personal experience, allowed a vanguard of young northern white men and women to respond to black initiatives for freedom with a concern that transcended self-interest. These young reformers, who became immediate abolitionists during the 1830s, developed considerable empathy for those in bondage [201]. They often invoked the biblical injunction to 'remember those in bonds as bound with them' [216 *p. 9*].

Revolutionary ideology played a continuing role in the ability of a few to empathize with a people whom most white Americans regarded as very different from themselves, inherently inferior, and well suited for enslavement. More profound influences, however, included a remarkable modernization of the northern economy – the Market Revolution – and a resurgence of evangelicalism – the Second Great Awakening.

By the early 1830s canals, steamboats, macadamized roads, and the first railroads were transforming the North. As the commercial network they formed expanded, an economy that had been based on self-sufficient farms, handcrafted products of independent craftsmen, and local markets gave way to one characterized by commercial farms, factories, and a national market [164]. Simultaneously, the North became more closely tied economically to a cotton-producing South with which it was increasingly unlike culturally [219].

As factory production expanded, growing numbers of northern men found employment as wage laborers. Wage labor more than any other single factor transformed northern values. While Americans had earlier regarded wage workers as dependents similar to slaves – and some workingmen's advocates continued to do so – by the 1830s most northerners regarded the wage-labor system as the linchpin of individual freedom. They assumed that those who worked for wages controlled their own destiny and could advance to become self-employed entrepreneurs. In contrast, the coerced labor of slaves, who had no incentive to improve themselves, seemed outmoded and barbaric [41].

Of particular significance in drawing whites to immediatism was the impact of the Market Revolution on the northern concept of family life. As men left home and farm to compete for wages and advancement, they sanctified the family as a refuge for religious and feminine virtue. Within the middle class, a cult of domesticity flourished that recognized women's pre-eminence as nurturers of children, repositories of Christian morality, and comforters of husbands.

Most northern families did not achieve in practice such a refined version of feminine domesticity. Working-class women could not devote themselves exclusively to their homes. But the idealized northern concept of family life made the condition of black families in southern slavery all the more shocking. That slaveholders could sexually violate slave mothers and rip away their children as commodities in the domestic slave trade provided ample motivation for white northerners, who invested so much emotion in their own family relations, to take up the antislavery cause. This was especially the case among evangelical Christians who were encouraged to engage in benevolent activities [41, 185].

In fact, while the Market Revolution created a disposition among northerners and some white residents of the border South to regard slavery as outmoded, barbaric, and immoral, it was the religious revival known as the Second Great Awakening that shaped a band of white men and women who advocated interracial action against human bondage. The sort of Christian engagement preached by Charles G. Finney, Lyman Beecher, and other revivalists of that era created a broad commitment to benevolent reform within which a radical antislavery movement could flourish [58, 222]. Only a small minority of white evangelicals became immediate abolitionists, because it required personal interaction with African Americans to arouse such a commitment. But, since evangelicalism thrived among northern blacks as well as whites, it provided an interracial reform vocabulary that facilitated such interaction by bridging racial differences [96, 185].

THE BENEVOLENT EMPIRE

Like their eighteenth-century predecessors, the revivalists of the 1820s and 1830s concentrated on redeeming individual sinners. They called on the sanctified to serve the coming kingdom of God as missionaries to such nonchristian portions of the world as China and Africa. They also focused on an American society cut loose from its traditional ethical moorings by the Market Revolution. Modernization had created in the North both opportunities for material advancement and worries that worldly success could be detrimental to one's salvation unless that success were combined with Christian benevolence. Objects for such benevolence were close at hand in what appeared to be rampant sabbath breaking, heathenism, prostitution, intemperance, gambling, crime, inhumanity, ignorance, and poverty. Many pious Yankees added the Democratic party to this list of evils. Organized during the 1820s and headed by unchurched dualist Andrew Jackson, the party seemed to foster a variety of vices among poor men who voted for its candidates [61, 110, 191].

From the time of the Puritans during the seventeenth century, New Englanders had believed America had a special role in the unfolding of God's providence. Therefore the righteous reaction during the early nineteenth century to social dislocation and apparent infidelity was strongest in that region. Similar sentiments flourished in Yankee communities located in western New York and northeastern Ohio [38, 185]. Reform activity extended into other portions of the North and into the South as well [151]. But it was evangelical New Englanders and persons of New England descent who became leaders in a variety of reform organizations, known collectively as the Benevolent Empire.

Such organizations appeared during the 1810s and increased their activities during the succeeding decades. Among the more influential of them were the American Board of Commissioners for Foreign Missions (1810), the American Bible Society (1816), the American Sunday School Union (1824), the American Tract Society (1816), and the American Peace Society (1828) [186]. Other societies embraced such causes as temperance, prison reform, aiding the physically and mentally impaired, or protecting sailors from brutal punishments. Not least among such organizations was the ACS. Like the others, it sought a moderate, broadly acceptable means for dealing with one of the nation's sins. It was, nevertheless, exceptional in its recognition that white northerners shared responsibility with white southerners for the evils associated with slavery.

WILLIAM LLOYD GARRISON

The individual responsible for uniting white northern evangelical reform with a more radical anti-colonizationist black abolitionism was William Lloyd Garrison. Garrison, who is regarded as the greatest of the American abolitionists, was born at Newburyport, Massachusetts in 1805. He was a son of a pious Baptist mother and an alcoholic, seafaring father who deserted his family in 1808. Deeply influenced by his mother's determination to advance the cause of righteousness, Garrison was well prepared for an age of reform. Just as important, his youthful apprenticeship to a printer shaped his career as a journalist schooled in the contentious newspaper business of his time. By January 1828, Garrison was editor of the *National Philanthropist*, a Boston temperance weekly, which criticized Sunday mail deliveries, lotteries, war, and dandified styles in men's clothing [123, 175, 177].

A few months later Garrison met Benjamin Lundy when this energetic Quaker abolitionist visited Boston. Lundy, who published his weekly *Genius of Universal Emancipation* in the slaveholding city of Baltimore, was a transitional figure in the antislavery cause. A white advocate of gradual emancipation who was not hostile to the ACS, Lundy nevertheless challenged slavery on its own ground throughout the 1820s. As the decade advanced, his denunciation of slaveholders became increasingly harsh and his association with free black abolitionists increasingly close, especially in helping those illegally held in slavery [64]. Lundy convinced Garrison that slavery was *the* American 'national sin' and persuaded Garrison to join him in Baltimore in September 1829 as co-editor of the *Genius* [175 p. 42].

Before he left Boston, Garrison had begun to formulate a new, more radical approach to the slavery issue that rested on a vision of equality within a biracial American community. He asserted that slaves were Americans by birth and entitled to the same rights enjoyed by whites. He called on whites to empathize with blacks, to imagine what it would be like to be enslaved, and to appreciate the terrible anger of African Americans against their oppressors. The country's churches and national government, he charged, had fallen under the sway of remorseless slaveholders and had involved northerners as well as southerners in a crime that begged divine punishment. Unless whites emancipated the slaves, he warned, blacks would rise up violently to seize their freedom. 'Blood will flow like water', he predicted, '... There will be heard lamentations and weeping, such as will blot out the remembrance of the horrors of St. Domingo [Haiti]' [38 *p. 145*].

By the time he reached Baltimore, Garrison had broken with the ACS and called for the immediate, uncompensated emancipation of the slaves without expatriation [38, 175]. His experience in that city strengthened him in this resolve as he began a long collaboration with black abolitionists. He and Lundy lived at the same boarding house with two black opponents of the ACS, William Watkins and Jacob Greener. Along with a young black man named Hezekiah Grice, Watkins and Greener strengthened Garrison in his opposition to the ACS by portraying it as both racist and proslavery in its view that there was no place for free blacks in the United States [89].

It was also in Baltimore that Garrison read David Walker's *Appeal*, which supported his contention that unless whites quickly brought about peaceful emancipation blacks would resort to revolutionary violence. Unlike other white antislavery advocates, Garrison – while rejecting violence – praised Walker's 'bravery and intelligence' and regarded him as representing black manhood [38 *p. 147*].

Garrison's direct observation of the brutality of slavery, his confrontations with slave traders, and his brief imprisonment in Baltimore Jail on charges of libeling one of the traders increased his empathy for the enslaved. He extended his sympathy to captured fugitive slaves he met in jail and reflected that his imprisonment was insignificant in comparison to the lifelong loss of freedom imposed on African Americans.

Following his release in June 1830, Garrison launched a speaking tour in the Northeast designed to spread his concept of immediate abolitionism. He was not the first advocate of immediatism, but he was the first to link it with a demand for black equality. Garrison, like most other white abolitionists, was stiff and condescending in his relations with African Americans. He failed to bring blacks into antislavery organizations on an equal basis with whites, yet he laid the groundwork for a more radical abolitionist movement by addressing integrated audiences and calling on whites to regard the slaves as their brothers and sisters [38].

Beyond African Americans, Quakers, and a small but extremely influential band of evangelical whites, Garrison initially made few converts. But, with the financial support of wealthy black Philadelphia abolitionist James Forten, he began publishing his weekly *Liberator* in Boston in January 1831. In what is perhaps the most famous editorial in American history, Garrison told his readers, sixty percent of whom were black, 'Urge me not to use moderation in a cause like the present. I am in earnest – I will not equivocate – I will not excuse – I will not retreat a single inch – AND I WILL BE HEARD' [*Doc. 5*].

THE AMERICAN ANTI-SLAVERY SOCIETY

Although some historians have described Garrison and other immediatists as extreme individualists [72], they were inveterate organizers who created powerful institutions aimed at spreading antislavery sentiment in the North and challenging the existence of slavery in the South. Garrison initiated immediatist organization during the autumn of 1831 when he and twelve other white men began the New England Anti-Slavery Society (NEASS), which quickly became biracial in its composition [89]. But the most important abolitionist organization of the 1830s was the American Anti-Slavery Society (AASS). With its executive office in New York City, the AASS employed traveling speakers, distributed documents, published the weekly *Emancipator*, and coordinated petition drives and postal campaigns.

The beginnings of the AASS lay in the first Black National Convention, which was held in Philadelphia in June 1831. Black abolitionists had invited Garrison, Lundy, and several other whites to attend this meeting and together they determined to initiate a national immediatist organization. But the furor caused by Nat Turner's rebellion delayed the organizational meeting of the AASS until December 1833. Turner's revolt also helped shape the society's character [63].

Throughout the antebellum period the antislavery movement was composed of regional leadership clusters and this was already clear that December when sixty-two individuals assembled in Philadelphia to form the AASS [87]. Twenty-one were Quakers, most of whom were from Pennsylvania. Another group, headed by wealthy New York City business-men Arthur and Lewis Tappan, consisted of orthodox evangelicals who had close ties to the Benevolent Empire. Beriah Green headed a similar evangelical contingent from western New York, while Garrison led a diverse group of New Englanders. There were only three black men – Robert Purvis, James G. Barbadoes, and James C. McCrummell – and four women – all of whom were white Quakers – in attendance. What was remarkable and daring was that there were any African Americans or women present at all [65, 176].

The society's Declaration of Sentiments called for immediate emancipation without 'expatriation' and for securing 'to the colored population of the United States, all rights and privileges which belong to them as men, and as Americans' [33 *p. 81, 83*]. The strong Quaker presence, Garrison's commitment to emulating Jesus Christ, and the furor aroused by Turner's recent rebellion led those in attendance to renounce explicitly 'all carnal weapons for deliverance from bondage' and to urge the slaves to do likewise. The participants committed themselves to abolish slavery through 'the potency of truth,' 'the power of love,' and 'the spirit of repentance' [*Doc. 6*].

From the start, however, abolitionists were ambivalent concerning the use of force in a righteous cause [87]. While calling for peaceful means, the Declaration also recognized that the American Revolution set a precedent for war against 'oppressors' [*Doc. 6*]. The brutality of slavery, the revolutionary tradition, the violence abolitionists faced, and the American concept of manhood all strained against a nonviolent doctrine.

The AASS used peaceful 'moral suasion' to spread immediatist views across the North. Abolitionists soon organized state societies in New England, New York, Pennsylvania, and in the Old Northwest. In some instances African Americans and women participated in these societies, in others they formed auxiliaries, and in yet others they did both [108, 149]. By 1837 there were 145 local societies in Massachusetts, 274 in New York, and 213 in Ohio. Many of the societies were small, but by 1838 the AASS claimed 1,350 affiliates and a membership of 250,000 [76].

During this period the most notable of the abolitionist agents was Theodore Dwight Weld, who was a disciple of Charles G. Finney and had close ties to the Tappan brothers. In 1834 Weld organized the famous student debate at Lane Theological Seminary in Cincinnati. For eighteen evenings the students weighed the merits of colonization against those of immediatism and decided almost unanimously in favor of immediatism. Soon after, a majority of the Lane students – all of whom were white – organized an antislavery society, opened schools for black children, and began interacting socially with the local black community.

The seminary's administrators reacted by expelling Weld and the other student abolitionists, who then moved to recently established Oberlin College in northeastern Ohio. They transformed Oberlin into an important center of biracial abolitionism in the Old Northwest. The expulsion also enabled Weld to organize a band of young white antislavery agents known as the 'Seventy,' who toured northern Ohio and western New York during 1835 and 1836 [37 *p. 154*, 118].

Meanwhile immediatists attempted to spread antislavery sentiment in the South and used petitions to introduce the issue in Congress. In 1835 the AASS's executive committee, under the leadership of Lewis Tappan, initiated an ambitious postal campaign designed to send southward huge amounts of antislavery literature. This sort of moral suasion sought to arouse antislavery sentiment among southern whites and convince repentant slaveholders to emancipate their slaves [*Docs. 7–8*]. But white southerners, fearing that such literature would reach free blacks and slaves, reacted to the postal campaign with anger. A mob burned abolitionist publications that reached Charleston, South Carolina. The United States Post Master encouraged southerners to withhold delivery of abolitionist mailings. President Andrew Jackson and several southern state legislatures called on northern states to suppress abolitionism [191, 237].

The petitioning effort faced similar resistance from proslavery forces but strengthened abolitionism in the North. Petitioning had long been a part of the movement. Black and white abolitionists had appealed to state legislatures during the 1770s. By the 1820s petitioning of Congress for action against slavery in the District of Columbia had become common [79]. With the advent of the AASS, petition campaigns served to bring nonabolitionist northerners into the antislavery effort as well as to raise the slavery issue in a national forum.

In reaction to a growing number of antislavery petitions, southern members of the House of Representatives – with significant northern support – succeeded in passing the Gag Rule in 1836. This House rule provided that petitions related to slavery would not be read; instead they would be automatically tabled without debate. The result was a controversy that highlighted a threat posed by slaveholders to the constitutional right of northern whites to petition Congress. Massachusetts Congressman John Quincy Adams, a former United States president, emphasized this point in his long – and by 1844 successful – struggle to repeal the Gag Rule. Supported by Whig Congressmen Joshua R. Giddings of Ohio, Seth M. Gates of western New York, and William Slade of Vermont, Adams established what amounted to an antislavery caucus in Congress [134, 155]. Meanwhile Joshua Leavitt, editor of the *Emancipator*, and Weld created an antislavery lobby in Washington, which continued to exist until the eve of the Civil War [101].

The abolitionists paid a heavy physical and emotional price for these labors. The testimony offered by Weld, the 'Seventy', and other black and white northern abolitionists, who became itinerant speakers in favor of emancipation and racial justice, often evoked violent responses. Mobs attacked Weld numerous times and his associate Marius Robinson was nearly beaten to death [37, 101, 121]. In 1837, at Alton, Illinois, rioters killed abolitionist journalist Elijah P. Lovejoy as he defended his press [*Doc. 9*]. Other abolitionist newspaper editors, such as James G. Birney and Gamaliel Bailey – both of the Cincinnati *Philanthropist* – lost presses to mobs during waves of antiabolitionist, anti-black rioting in the urban North [99, 154]. Abolitionists who dared to venture into the South faced whipping and arrest.

THE BREAK-UP OF THE AASS

Antiabolitionist violence, failure of the postal campaign, and the tendency of northern whites to oppose slavery only to the extent of its infringement on their own rights each contributed to the break-up of the AASS between 1838 and 1840.

Garrison and his New England associates reacted to the failure of Americans to respond adequately to moral suasion by determining that slavery was merely the worst sin in a nation so corrupt that it required a profound cultural and political – though not economic – restructuring. Increasingly focused on northern injustice, Garrisonians championed women's rights, grew antagonistic to orthodox Christianity, and endorsed an anarchistic doctrine called *nonresistance*, which condemned all human government as resting immorally on force. By 1843 they were denouncing the United States Constitution as irrevocably proslavery and maintaining that the North must dissolve the Union in order to terminate its sinful and criminal support of slavery in the South [230].

Other abolitionist leadership clusters, however, produced different strategies for advancing the antislavery cause. Louis Tappan's group of orthodox evangelicals hoped it could yet use churches as antislavery instruments. While Tappan and his church-oriented associates were leery of politics, they were not nonresistants and regarded disunion as tantamount to abandoning the slaves to the masters. They were also far more traditional in their views concerning the role of women than were most Garrisonians, although certainly more liberal in that regard than most of their contemporaries [87, 125].

Meanwhile, in the intensely evangelized Burnt-over District of western New York, abolitionists led by Alvan Stewart, Myron Holley, and Beriah Green laid the foundations for what became known as 'righteous government' [9(a)]. Interpreting the United States Constitution as an antislavery document, these radical political abolitionists advocated the creation of an abolitionist political party committed to ending slavery in the southern states. Believing that divine and natural law made it impossible for human law legitimately to protect slavery, they joined black abolitionists in helping slaves escape [102, 187, 216].

Finally, another group of abolitionists, formed in Cincinnati around Gamaliel Bailey, Democratic United States Senator Thomas Morris, and – by 1842 – Salmon P. Chase, a pious local attorney who joined the antislavery movement in response to antiabolitionist violence. The Cincinnati abolitionists advocated political action against slavery within the national domain – in the District of Columbia, in interstate commerce, in the territories – while maintaining the common assumption of the era that slavery in the southern states was beyond the reach of central government power. In this the Cincinnati group had much in common with antislavery politicians such as Adams, Giddings, Slade, and Gates [48, 101].

Yet the Cincinnati cluster of abolitionists, located just across the Ohio River from slaveholding Kentucky, did not intend to leave slavery alone where it existed in the South. Bailey and Chase combined their recognition of state control over slavery with efforts to spread political abolitionism into the upper South. This approach appealed to such southern white abolitionists as Cassius M. Clay and John G. Fee of Kentucky, Joseph Evans Snodgrass of Maryland, and Samuel M. Janney of Virginia [102]. Largely because of the physical distance separating the Cincinnati group from eastern abolitionist centers, it was on the periphery of the disagreements that rocked the movement during the late 1830s.

The central controversies that split the AASS were those involving the relationship of abolitionists to the nation's churches, the feasibility and morality of an abolitionist political party, and the status of women at antislavery meetings. Garrison's strongly worded criticisms of the churches for failing to condemn slaveholding as sinful and his heterodox religious views – including Christian perfectionism and antisabbatarianism – disturbed clergy and many orthodox lay people among the immediatists [115].

Many abolitionists also shared the common belief that to allow women to act like men in public meetings was dangerous to the social order and antithetic to the role of women as virtuous keepers of homes and nurturers of children. Orthodox evangelical abolitionists not only felt threatened but feared that the increasing radicalism of Garrison and his associates would alienate potential converts to immediatism. Meanwhile Garrisonians, who hoped to influence the Whig and Democratic parties, clashed with the radical political abolitionists who determined that they could no longer rely on sinfully proslavery parties to advance antislavery goals [115].

The first signs of trouble arose in 1837 when clerical abolitionists, including Henry B. Stanton, Elizur Wright Jr, and Charles T. Torrey, unsuccessfully challenged Garrison within the Massachusetts Anti-Slavery Society (MASS) on the issues of religious orthodoxy and women's participation in the society's meetings. By 1839 the political issue and the 'woman question' caused dissension at the annual meetings of the MASS and the AASS.

Defeated overwhelmingly at the MASS meeting, Stanton, Torrey, and others withdrew from that organization to form a separate Massachusetts Abolition Society. At the AASS meeting that year, while Garrisonians secured the right of women to vote, neither side won a clear victory on the issue of political tactics. Consequently, both Garrisonians and their opponents attempted to pack the 1840 AASS convention in New York City with their supporters. The Garrisonians prevailed and, when they elected a woman – Abigail Kelley – to the convention's business committee, Lewis Tappan led the evangelicals out of the organization [166, 175].

This left the Garrisonians in control of the much diminished AASS. Henceforth the Garrisonians represented a decided minority among abolitionists, while remaining influential propagandists, effective critics of political abolitionists, and gages of antislavery opinion in the North. They were hampered, however, by their interpretation of the United States Constitution as a proslavery document, which prevented them from effectively challenging the existence of slavery in the South, by their disinclination to aid in underground railroad operations, and by their tendency toward abstraction [102, 215].

As it turned out after 1840, new abolitionist organizations that were philosophically less radical than the AASS were more radical in their practical impact on the sectional struggle. Lewis Tappan deserves much of the credit for this. He led in creating the American and Foreign Anti-Slavery

Society (AFASS), which from 1840 until 1855 struggled to abolitionize the major Christian denominations while supporting those abolitionists who determined to withdraw from – or come out of – what they considered to be proslavery churches [125]. Tappan was also in 1846 the primary creator of the American Missionary Association (AMA). This alternative to pro-slavery missionary groups became the largest antebellum abolitionist organization and the most active supporter of evangelical opponents of slavery in the South [62, 102, 191].

The most prominent of the 'comeouter' churches were the Wesleyan Methodists, who broke with the Methodist Episcopal Church in 1842, the American Baptist Free Mission Society that formed in 1845, and the Free Presbyterians who were organized by John Rankin in 1846. These religious organizations provided thousands of dedicated grassroots abolitionist activists during the 1840s, 1850s, and 1860s [126, 186, 223].

Meanwhile the radical political abolitionists initiated the Liberty party as an abolitionist third party in 1840. Among the group's leaders were Myron Holley, Gerrit Smith, James G. Birney, Charles T. Torrey, Joshua Leavitt, Alvan Stewart, and William L. Chaplin, most of whom lived in western New York. Their view of the Constitution as an antislavery document, their commitment to helping slaves escape, and their dawning support for antislavery violence made them the vanguard in aggressive abolitionism. But just as influential were less militant Liberty abolitionists, such as Gamaliel Bailey and Salmon P. Chase, who sought to create a broad-based antislavery party that could spread political abolitionism into the South itself [48, 101, 102, 166].

CHAPTER FOUR

ABOLITIONISTS AND GENDER

The role of gender in the American antislavery movement was complex and dynamic. Immediate abolitionism during the 1830s was the direct precursor of the women's rights movement begun at Seneca Falls, New York in 1848. With considerable male support, women participated in every phase of abolitionism – organization, moral suasion, political action, and helping slaves escape. Not only did many male abolitionists encourage an expanded social role for women, they often embraced a feminized version of masculinity, which led them to endorse – with various levels of consistency – cooperation over competition, forgiveness over retribution, and nonviolence over violence. Even so, female abolitionists occupied a separate and subordinate position within the antislavery movement through the 1830s. With some notable exceptions among Garrisonians, this continued to be the case during the 1840s and 1850s, although women expanded their involvement among all antislavery factions during those decades.

WOMEN AND ANTISLAVERY BEFORE THE FORMATION OF THE AASS

Black and white women took part in antislavery activities during the eighteenth century and the first decades of the nineteenth century. Many enslaved black women took direct action against slavery, while a very few black and white women used superior social standing to enunciate antislavery principles.

From the time of the New York City uprising in 1712, black women sought freedom. Some violently resisted enslavement through escape and rebellion, although in lesser numbers than black men [136]. Others initiated court suits seeking emancipation or became practical abolitionists who purchased freedom for themselves and others. During the 1780s, Elizabeth Freeman, a Massachusetts slave, initiated a freedom suit based on a clause in that state's new constitution recognizing the universality of natural rights. Freeman's suit not only resulted in her own freedom but contributed to a state supreme court decision abolishing slavery within its jurisdiction. More common, however, were individuals like Alethia Tanner of Washington, DC, who during the 1810s and 1820s purchased her own freedom, her sister's, and the freedom of her sister's ten children and five grandchildren [181, 198].

No women – either black or white – participated in the gradual abolition societies of the Revolutionary Era. But several women of that time advocated universal liberty. In 1774, Abigail Adams, the wife of Patriot leader John Adams, responded to black protest in Massachusetts by telling her husband, 'It always seemed a most iniquitous scheme to me to fight ourselves for what we are daily robbing and plundering from those who have as good a right to freedom as we have' [104 *p. 56*]. A few years later, the African-born poet Phillis Wheatley declared in a letter, 'In every human breast, God has implanted a Principle, which we call love of freedom; it is impatient of Oppression, and pants for Deliverance' [138 *p. 58*]. Both Adams and Wheatley expressed these antislavery sentiments in the North and in private. But, in 1791, a white woman known only as Sister White-head publicly informed a group of Methodist ministers assembled in South Carolina that their support of slavery contradicted the doctrines of Christianity. 'O! my Lord,' she exclaimed, 'is this the religion of my adorable master Jesus?' [73 *p. 63*].

By the late 1820s and early 1830s two women were helping to shape immediate abolitionism in America. They were Elizabeth Chandler, a white Quaker from Delaware, and Maria W. Stewart, a black widow from Boston. Chandler wrote a women's column for Benjamin Lundy's *Genius of Universal Emancipation* and later organized antislavery women in Phila-delphia and Michigan. She emphasized the capacity of women for moral leadership and sought to develop empathy among northern women for suffering black families. Referring to black women in slavery, Chandler reminded her white audience, 'their cause is our cause – they are one with us in sex and nature – a portion of ourselves' [96 *p. 190*]. Following Chandler's untimely death at age twenty-six in 1834, Lundy and Garrison contended that she was the first woman to concentrate her energies on behalf of the enslaved.

Stewart had an even briefer antislavery career than Chandler but was equally influential in developing themes that defined immediatism. Directly influenced by David Walker, Stewart addressed a black masonic lodge in 1833 when she was twenty-six, urging those assembled to be more courageous in asserting the rights of their race. Her stinging words combined with her audacious violation of her womanly sphere led to a backlash against her within Boston's black community that drove her out of the city and out of public speaking. But her admonition that black women must 'strive, by their example both in public and private' to assist in the antislavery struggle took root among black northern women who were already forming abolitionist auxiliaries [104 *p. 176*].

SEPARATE SPHERES AND IMMEDIATISM

The few northern – and fewer southern – women who became immediate abolitionists during the 1830s did so within a cultural context epitomized by the doctrine of separate social spheres for men and women. The doctrine reflected traditional patriarchal values, holding that men had an inherent right to rule, and a perception that there were essential differences between the abilities of men and women. It, nevertheless, recognized a significant degree of autonomy for the latter gender [57].

During the early nineteenth century Americans believed aggressiveness, bravery, physical strength, and intelligence to be masculine attributes. They suited men to excel in business, war, the professions, and politics. In contrast, 'true women' surpassed men in the Christian virtues of piety, sexual purity, domesticity, and submissiveness. It followed that a woman's place was in the home, where she bore, raised, and provided religious instruction to children, performed domestic duties, and provided her husband with a gentle respite from the strife-filled manly world [195 *p. 40*]. Religious leaders who dominated popular opinion feared that disruption of the social balance created by this sexual division of labor would destroy civilization.

This outlook was most prevalent among well-to-do white families and it denigrated black and working-class white women who did not meet its prerequisites. But it also shaped the values of the free African-American elite and the working-class families of both races who strove for *respectability*. The Market Revolution, which required many northern men to spend their working days away from home, contributed to the force of the doctrine. So did a patriarchal reaction against expanding opportunities for women beyond the domestic sphere. Yet the concept also reflected romantic values in its respect for female emotion and intuition. By according women authority in areas of religion, morality, and child-rearing, it provided a bridge that a small minority of women were able to cross into reform, abolitionism, and feminism [87, 186, 195].

Both the American Revolution and the Market Revolution produced expanded opportunities for women to gain education and confidence in their abilities. Although no women could vote or engage directly in politics, white women at least were expected during the post-Revolutionary decades to raise boys for active citizenship and for that task the women themselves had to have education. By the late eighteenth century a variety of private academies for white women had come into existence across the North and upper South. Simultaneously, emancipation in the northern states and manumission in the Chesapeake led to growing numbers of free African

Americans, the more successful of whom sought to educate their daughters as well as their sons. In each case women received educations, grounded in Christian theology, that prepared them to think critically about the issues of their time.

Other women, both black and white, gained independence through employment. Young northern white women were among the first to earn wages in the textile industry. Free black women gained standing within their communities as seamstresses, caterers, teachers, and boarding-house operators, as well as domestic servants and washwomen. With economic independence, a growing minority of women of both races were able to delay or avoid marriage and define themselves in terms other than those of wife and mother [96, 195].

It was, nevertheless, recognition of feminine pre-eminence in matters of Christian morality and family life that led women to become reformers and abolitionists [183]. Women responded in greater numbers than men to revivalism and became active workers in the Benevolent Empire. Under male supervision, they participated in public reform meetings, raised money for missionary efforts and the ACS, and taught Sunday school [93, 96]. Since the 1790s black and white women had organized female benevolent societies on behalf of widows, orphans, and other unfortunates. This respectable moral activism among women, aimed at reinforcing established social values, gained universal praise [87, 96, 108].

Abolitionism, however, challenged the racial, political, moral, and social *status quo* and, therefore, was *not* respectable. It raised the specter of equal rights for despised African Americans and threatened sectional peace between the North and South. Especially during the 1830s, a woman who became an abolitionist risked social disgrace and mob violence, and – as was the case with men – few took the risk [96, 108, 183].

Because black churches had long engaged in practical antislavery efforts, because northern blacks often had family ties to those still in slavery, and because of distrust of the ACS within the black community, women of color were the first of their gender to embrace immediatism. In 1832 at Salem, Massachusetts, African Americans formed the first women's antislavery society in the United States [195].

It is more difficult to say what motivated the few white women who became immediatists. As was the case with white men, New England descent, involvement in the Benevolent Empire, association with African Americans, and disillusionment with the ACS were important factors. Like their male counterparts, white antislavery women tended to be young – often unmarried – and in quest of meaning for their lives. Antislavery ministers, friends, family members, and Garrison, who in January 1832 began explicit appeals to women, influenced their choices [96, 108, 183].

Most important, the doctrine of True Womanhood encouraged them to be sensitive to issues of morality affecting families. As it became clear that there could be no 'sanctity of the home' [96 *p. 216*] for slaves nor chastity for enslaved women, conscience drove a few white women to embrace immediatism. Seeking to establish empathy, members of the Portland (Maine) Female Anti-Slavery Society in 1838 asked each other to envision a slave woman nursing her baby 'with the dread of the driver's whip before her eyes' [108 *p. 69*].

Even before Garrison began appealing for their support, women helped organize the AASS. Quaker preacher Lucretia Mott of Philadelphia and three other women attended the initial meeting of the society in December 1831. In a marked departure from custom, Mott spoke briefly at the meeting and the men in attendance responded favorably [87]. This began a four-decades-long association of abolitionism and efforts on the part of women to transcend traditional gender roles. Mott, who had close ties to black abolitionists, became one of the more active leaders in the antislavery cause. For over three decades, she preached in Maryland, Virginia, and the District of Columbia as well as in the North against slavery [96, 102].

Other white women emerged as prominent abolitionists during the decades that followed. Among white females there were New Englanders Maria Weston Chapman and Lydia Maria Child, who served along with Mott as members of the AASS executive committee during the 1840s and 1850s [146]. An accomplished author, Child for several years during the early 1840s edited the society's weekly *National Anti-Slavery Standard* [113]. Chapman led the Boston Female Anti-Slavery Society and edited abolitionist periodicals. There was also Abigail Kelley, who became Abigail Kelley Foster when she married Stephen S. Foster in 1845. An AASS agent who was extremely abrasive in her denunciation of northern churches and Liberty party supporters, Foster was active in New York and Ohio as well as Massachusetts [87, 171].

Chapman, Child, and Foster were all Garrisonians. But Jane Grey Swisshelm, who published an antislavery newspaper in Pittsburgh, Myrtilla Miner, who established a school for black girls in Washington, DC, and numerous other women cooperated with antislavery groups less committed to women's rights. These groups included the AFASS and such political organizations as the Liberty, Free Soil and Republican parties [2, 104, 188].

A number of black women also rose to prominence as abolitionists. Former New York slave and evangelical preacher Sojourner Truth, who became an active abolitionist during the late 1840s, was the most powerful speaker among them [143, *Doc. 15*]. But others, such as Mary Ann Shadd Cary, an advocate of black settlement in Canada, Frances Ellen Watkins Harper, an agent of the Pennsylvania Anti-Slavery Society and of the Maine Anti-Slavery Society, and Sarah Remond of New York, who often worked with white abolitionist women, were very influential. During the 1850s

Cary became the first black woman to edit a newspaper, when she assumed responsibility for the *Provincial Freeman* in Toronto [108, 149, 195].

Yet recognizing the prominence of a few women in abolitionism can be misleading. Female and male abolitionists of both races only slowly broke with prevailing notions concerning the social segregation and subordination of women [87]. Although there were some local mixed-gender antislavery societies, women generally maintained their own organizations as auxiliaries to those controlled by men [160]. Even within their separate organizations, it was difficult for antislavery women not to defer to men. When Mott and others established the Philadelphia Female Anti-Slavery Society (PFASS) in 1833, for example, they requested a man – black abolitionist James McCrummell – to preside and had men give the principal addresses. Women's societies during the 1830s elected men to represent them at state and national antislavery meetings [183].

Women abolitionists were also very conscious of tension between their antislavery activism and what was expected of respectable 'ladies'. In early 1837, the PFASS declared, 'We will never overstep the boundaries of propriety, but when our brothers and sisters, lie crushed and bleeding ... we must do with our might, what our hands find to do ... pausing only to inquire, "What is right?"' [108 *p. 69*]. Trained to follow and plagued by feelings of inadequacy, women had especial difficulty assuming leadership roles. But slowly leaders emerged, as did an emphasis on efficiency, energy, and action. Women also gained a sense of feminist community within the context of abolitionism. They perceived themselves to be a band of activists apart from other women [87, 108].

The principal formal task of women's auxiliaries was raising money to be expended by the male-dominated societies. Women sewed to raise money for fugitive slaves, held raffles, organized bazaars and fairs. They also provided most of the labor in circulating petitions. By the early 1840s, female abolitionists had begun distributing Liberty party campaign material to voters [108, 183]. In their labor on behalf of petition efforts and the Liberty party, antislavery women approached the borders of political engagement.

ABOLITIONIST MASCULINITY

Just as an emerging feminism among abolitionist women existed in tension with prevailing notions of separate spheres, the masculinity of black and white northern male abolitionists was under considerable stress. Southern concepts of manhood remained constant throughout the antebellum era. Men in the South defined themselves in terms of social hierarchy, patriarchy, and honor acquired through family standing, land ownership, fighting, drinking, womanizing, and prideful display [192].

But the Market Revolution and the Second Great Awakening splintered concepts of masculinity in the North. The Market Revolution encouraged a male ethos based on commercial acquisitiveness and individualism, as well as on traditional regard for forceful action, sexual prowess, and alcohol consumption [228]. The Second Great Awakening shaped an alternative masculine ideal influenced by a feminization of religious experience. Piety and rejection of such things as extramarital sexual activity, consumption of alcoholic beverages, and resort to violence became standards of manhood among 'Christian gentlemen' [206 *p. 213*]. Although they did not abjure commercial acquisitiveness, such individuals embraced the feminine virtues of compassion and empathy. They believed benevolence to be a manly duty.

Directly influenced by these values, William Lloyd Garrison and other abolitionists called on men to reject pride and ambition in favor of love, joy, peace, gentleness, goodness, faith, meekness, and temperance [238]. Male abolitionists developed emotional relationships among themselves based on what they perceived to be womanly virtues of cooperation, forgiveness, self-sacrifice, and intimacy. Garrisonian men greeted each other with kisses on the cheek. They often held hands. Other male abolitionists sometimes acted similarly and were to varying degrees appreciative of the strengths of antislavery women [194].

Nevertheless, while they consciously embraced a feminized version of manhood, male abolitionists retained an emotional allegiance to traditional concepts of masculine honor. An evangelical determination to be Christ-like contributed to their decisions to become abolitionists. They associated Christ with the feminine qualities of a loving, nonviolent, and submissive saviour and they contrasted such values with the sinful, violent, and oppressive system of slavery. But it was clear from the start that when northern men became immediatists they did not reject confrontation nor give up their admiration of violent displays of courage [193, 238].

In other words, there were limits to male abolitionist admiration for feminine values and willingness to accept women as equals in the anti-slavery struggle. Despite their endorsement of peaceful means and – in some cases – nonresistance, black and white northern male abolitionists valued confrontation and shared their culture's respect for heroes engaged in righteous violence [102, 126]. During the 1830s such abolitionists as James G. Birney, Arthur Tappan, and the martyred Elijah P. Lovejoy resorted to firearms in defense of the antislavery cause [121, *Doc. 9*]. While some northern abolitionists criticized Kentucky abolitionist Cassius M. Clay for his use of 'cold steel' in self-defense during the 1840s, others admired his heroism [102 *p. 136*]. Black and white abolitionists took pride in their violent resistance to slavecatchers and those who tried to kidnap free African Americans into slavery.

There was a Puritan-style militancy among male – and some female –

abolitionists that was confrontational rather than meek or peaceful. At an antislavery meeting held in New York City in 1850 Garrison and his colleague Wendell Phillips forcefully asserted their masculine superiority over a group of tough, working-class, proslavery hecklers. 'There is not a man among you,' Garrison yelled. 'If you have men of intellect, come up here on this platform. Pick out your man, if you have a man among you who dares to say "boo to a goose," which I very much doubt.' Phillips was bolder, calling the hecklers 'cringing wretches' and declaring 'we are able to protect ourselves, and we shall do so' [238 vol. 1, *p. 243*]. It is true that Harriet Beecher Stowe and others within the antislavery movement praised enslaved African Americans for what they perceived to be Christ-like submissiveness. But black abolitionists generally and such white abolitionists as John Brown and Thomas Wentworth Higginson disparaged what they regarded to be the feminine qualities of black men in slavery [102, 185].

Especially during the 1830s and 1840s, confrontational, violence-tinged conditions encouraged bonding among male abolitionists – just as sisterhood flourished among female abolitionists. As male abolitionists traveled together, ate together, slept together, and faced violent mobs together, they developed a considerable degree of intimacy among themselves. Years after he and white abolitionist William White suffered injuries at the hands of an antiabolitionist mob in Indiana, black abolitionist Frederick Douglass did not hesitate to express his love for White [124].

The shared hardships and dangers that encouraged male abolitionists to cultivate fellowship among themselves hampered what ability they had to recognize women as equal partners in the antislavery cause. It was not until the late 1840s and 1850s, when antislavery women had, through their separate organizations, gained confidence in themselves, that male abolitionists began to regard them 'as genuine colleagues' [87 *p. 141*]. Even then, gender remained an issue, because both female and male abolitionists continued to recognize what they regarded to be a peculiarly feminine moral strength and sensitivity.

ABOLITIONISM AND FEMINISM

It is fair to say that male abolitionists simultaneously encouraged and discouraged an expanded role for their female colleagues. Some, such as Garrison and Douglass, were far more willing to accord women equality within the antislavery movement than were others, such as Lewis Tappan and James G. Birney. Yet Tappan, Birney, and those abolitionists who agreed with them were more progressive in their regard for an expanded role for women than were most Americans of their time [87, 185]. In addition, not all antislavery women embraced feminism and those who modified their commitment to the doctrine of separate spheres did so gradually and never completely [196]. The women's rights movement was, nevertheless, a product of abolitionism [186].

It was out of women's antislavery societies, sewing circles, fairs, and petition campaigns that feminist sisterhood emerged. Such organizations and efforts produced a constituency for the women's rights movement and provided a training ground for feminist leaders. But it took several extraordinary individuals to crystalize the movement. Chief among them were the sisters Angelina and Sarah Grimké of South Carolina [87, 117].

Motivated by a religious desire to purify themselves from sin, first Sarah and then Angelina during the 1820s left their slaveholding family, settled in Philadelphia, and became Quakers. At first they supported the ACS, but under the influence of such black abolitionists as Sarah Douglass and Sarah Forten, whom they met in the city, they became immediatists [96, 183].

Angelina, who was also influenced by Garrison's *Liberator*, joined the PFASS in 1834 and in 1836 published her 'Appeal to the Christian Women of the Southern States' [*Doc. 8*]. She called on white southern women to take the lead in emancipation by persuading their male relatives 'that slavery is a crime *against* God *and man*' [183 p. 9]. Shortly thereafter the sisters, who had moved to New York City, found employment with the AASS as the first paid female antislavery lecturers in the United States. Coached as public speakers by Theodore D. Weld, who married Angelina in 1838, the Grimkés undertook a lecture tour that created an impression among men and women, friends and foes, that women were in the lead of the antislavery movement. Angelina became a riveting speaker who attracted men to her initially single-gender meetings and thereby set in motion a controversy that both disrupted the AASS and produced self-conscious feminism [96, 183, 186].

The Grimké sisters challenged the pervasive assumption among abolitionists and Americans generally that respectable women should never speak in public in any circumstances. Angelina sparked an uproar when she discussed – before sexually integrated audiences – the sexual abuse inflicted on enslaved black women by their masters [96]. It was the opening of this *indelicate* subject that led orthodox clergy to denounce Angelina's and Sarah's conduct as unbecoming their gender [183, 186].

The fierceness of the clerical reaction led the Grimkés and other abolitionist women to analyze how American culture limited their freedom. They did so in the context of what they knew about the oppression of African Americans in slavery. Lydia Maria Child noted, 'the comparison between [white] women and the colored race is striking ... both have been kept in subjection by physical force, and considered rather in the light of property, than as individuals' [186 p. 105]. In response to their critics, the Grimkés each wrote a pamphlet objecting to the subordination of women to men, asserting the right of women to an equal role in reform with men, and insisting that the genders have equal rights and duties [96].

Angelina's marriage to Weld, Sarah's decision to join their household, their involvement in child-rearing, and their declining health ended, by 1840, their active involvement in the antislavery movement. But by then hundreds of other abolitionist women, whose empathy with slaves made them aware of their own limited freedom, took up the cause of women's rights [87, 183]. As early as 1837 the Anti-Slavery Convention of American Women declared, 'The time has come for woman to move in that sphere which providence has assigned her, and no longer remain satisfied with the circumvented limits with which corrupt custom and a perverted application of Scripture have encircled her' [135 *p. 144*].

It was the Grimkés' public speaking, too, that began the controversy that served as the immediate cause of the disruption of the AASS in 1840. By 1837, Garrison and his associates who supported the Grimkés were becoming outspoken feminists. But clerical abolitionists and others – both female and male – continued to insist on separate spheres for men and women. They believed that a linkage of abolitionism and women's rights would weaken the antislavery movement.

While other issues were at least as important as women's rights in causing dissention within the AASS, the 'women question' became the flash point. Those such as Lewis Tappan, who wanted to abolitionize the churches, and those such as James G. Birney, who hoped to create an independent abolitionist party, feared that radical advocacy of women's rights would hamper their efforts. Therefore the election of Abigail Kelley to the AASS business committee in 1840 was the occasion for the break-up of the AASS rather than its cause. When church-oriented and political abolitionists left the AASS, women's antislavery societies also split into those who supported Garrison and those who sided with the new organizations [185, 197].

Even more significant for the women's rights movement was the World Anti-Slavery Convention held in London in June 1840. The American delegation to this British meeting included blacks and whites, men and women, and members of both the AASS and AFASS. As soon as the Americans arrived, the convention managers warned the seven female delegates that they would not be recognized and should sit in the gallery reserved for spectators. While Birney, who was representing the AFASS affiliated New York Ladies Anti-Slavery Society, remained silent, several Garrisonians, including Wendell Phillips and George Bradburn, argued that the women should be seated as delegates. When the convention voted overwhelmingly to exclude them, Garrison, Nathaniel P. Rogers, William Adams, and black abolitionist Charles Remond (all Garrisonians) joined the women in the gallery in order to demonstrate their support [79, 197].

Their experience in London led two American abolitionists – Elizabeth Cady Stanton and Lucretia Mott – to commit themselves to calling a women's rights convention when they returned to the United States. But it was not until 1848, when Mott traveled from Philadelphia to western New York on other business and decided to visit Stanton at her home in the village of Seneca Falls, that they actually issued their call. On very short notice, a total of nearly three hundred men and woman – the best known of whom was black abolitionist Frederick Douglass – attended the Seneca Falls meeting [124, *Doc. 14*]. Stanton, Mott, and four other women drafted a declaration of sentiments, which asserted that 'all men and women are created equal' and indicted men for undermining women's abilities and self-respect [186 *p. 107*]. The delegates unanimously passed resolutions demanding expanded educational and professional opportunities for women, more equitable laws for marriage and divorce, and a single standard of sexual morality.

Stanton's resolution calling for women to be granted the right to vote faced more opposition than these others at the convention. It was difficult for those Garrisonians who regarded voting to be sinful to support such a proposition. Also contending that white women should vote, at a time when most black men could not do so, threatened to strain relationships between white feminists and black abolitionists. Ironically, Douglass was the only man at the convention to favor this proposal and it passed narrowly only as a result of his support [124].

The chief impact of the Seneca Falls meeting was the initiation of a women's rights movement organizationally distinct from abolitionism. Local feminist groups appeared across the North, there were important 'national' meetings held in 1850 at Salem, Ohio and Worcester, Massachusetts. A feminist press emerged. But increasingly feminism undermined the commitment of white women to black rights [69, 186 *p. 108*, 195].

While the 1850s witnessed a general upsurge in interracial cooperation against slavery, the women's movement remained segregated [195]. There were no African-American women at Seneca Falls and Sojourner Truth was one of very few black women who regularly attended white women's meetings. This was not because white feminists feared being linked in the public mind with abolitionism – they were abolitionists themselves. Rather, many of them perceived black women, most of whom were poor, to be disreputable compared to themselves. Like others of both races, white feminists also tended to categorize black women with black men as victims of slavery rather than of sexism [197].

Yet there was a black feminist movement with origins parallel to those of white feminism. It began with Maria Stewart's challenge to separate spheres during the early 1830s when she urged black women to adopt male standards of behavior and to enter business. Truth, Mary Ann Shadd Cary, and other black women continued to press for recognition of women's rights in black venues during the 1840s, 1850s, and 1860s.

While some black male abolitionists were, like Douglass, sympathetic to these efforts, they generally believed that feminism should be subordinate to abolitionism. When the AASS split in 1840 many black male abolitionists – several of whom were members of the clergy – opposed the participation of women. Subsequently, they joined the AFASS and its offshoot the American Missionary Association (AMA). Throughout the 1840s and 1850s, black women who supported a feminist agenda also tended to give priority to abolition and worked – with mixed results – to achieve active membership at black antislavery gatherings [62, 195].

Historians have long been aware of the connection between abolitionism and feminism and of how issues of women's rights helped split the AASS. But only within the past three decades has the role of gender – both feminine and masculine – in abolitionism been closely studied. One reason for the upsurge in interest is that the vast writings of abolitionists are a fertile field for reaching an understanding of how concepts of masculinity and femininity shaped antebellum northern behavior in general. Another reason is that an appreciation of the role of gender helps us to understand better the antislavery movement itself. Realizing that opposition to slavery existed within the context of a revolution in concepts of gender relationships is key to understanding the nature of the movement. But it is also essential to understand that the emergence of new concepts of gender and changes within American abolitionism took place within a biracial social framework.

CHAPTER FIVE

ABOLITIONISTS AND RACE

When the AASS organized in 1833 it announced two goals. They were the immediate abolition of slavery and equal rights for African Americans in the United States [Doc. 6]. The immediatists thereby rejected gradual emancipation and the expatriation of former slaves. But what white abolitionists meant by racial equality, how they proposed to achieve it, and how their commitment to it changed over time are debatable issues. How black abolitionists perceived racial issues is at least as controversial.

THE ANTEBELLUM DEBATE OVER RACE

As immediatism emerged as a major social movement, several cultural and intellectual forces shaped the context within which black and white abolitionist conceptions of race and attitudes toward racial justice developed. Among those forces were increasing class stratification, scientific racism, and romanticism, all of which contributed to mounting racial divisions in the United States.

The Market Revolution made class a more visible factor in northern society. Urban laborers were often at the mercy of economic forces they could neither control nor fully understand. Meanwhile the well-to-do grew fearful of the laboring masses. These insecurities and fears frequently had negative effects on race relations.

By the 1820s working-class whites, who competed against blacks for jobs, were reacting against self-assertion within the North's urban African-American communities. Anti-black riots became increasingly common in northern cities. White working-class antipathy to African Americans also produced attempts in northern state legislatures to ban further black settlement and to restrict the rights of black people who were already residents. Colonizationist sentiment, maintaining that there was no place for blacks in America, gained strength [96, 156, 232].

When immediate abolitionists organized during the early 1830s, they inadvertently triggered an intensification of these racist tendencies among white northerners. White wage laborers feared that black advancement would come at their expense [156, 232]. Wealthy white 'gentlemen of property and standing' perceived immediatism to be a threat to the social order [154]. As a result, by the mid-1830s racial violence had become even more common in the North.

Meanwhile scientific racism challenged both biblical assertions of human unity and eighteenth-century environmental explanations of human diversity. What became known as the American School of Ethnology relied on skull measurements and archeology to maintain that black people constituted a separate, inherently inferior, brutal, and savage species [85, 170]. Pseudoscientists and proslavery ideologues contended that, under the firm control of benevolent masters, black people were childlike and content. But, they warned, under abolitionist influences the natural savagery of African Americans would surface. According to this scenario, African Americans, once free, were bound to plague the South with vicious racial warfare. Others claimed scientific support for the thesis that God had designed black, white, and other peoples for different climatic zones, so that racial separation was the natural condition of mankind [85, 87, 234].

Such contentions made it difficult for abolitionists to argue on behalf of black equality. On occasion they sidestepped the issue by maintaining that inferiority was no justification for enslavement, noting that Christ said the strong should help the weak, not oppress them [11]. More frequently they quoted the biblical passage affirming that God had created all nations of one blood and stood by environmentalism. If black people had not been subjected to the brutality of slavery, abolitionists insisted, their abilities and standards of morality would equal those of whites [185].

Still, abolitionists themselves often maintained that blacks were innately different from whites. They accepted the romantic notion of *volksgeist* – the assumption that each nationality had a unique spirit – and they applied this assumption to the principal racial groups in the United States. In a manner that now seems incredible, they ignored women in this racial theorizing except to the extent that they evaluated male racial characteristics according to degrees of femininity and masculinity.

What historian George M. Fredrickson calls 'romantic racialism' held that white or Anglo-Saxon men were more masculine than black men and that black men exhibited feminine characteristics [85 *pp. 97–129*]. Accordingly, Anglo-Saxon men were imagined to be typically intellectual, adventuresome, aggressive, exploitative, and militaristic. Men of African descent were portrayed as typically emotional, sedentary, submissive, generous, and peaceful.

Black men were, from this perspective, natural Christians more inclined to forgive their oppressors than rise up against them. 'The negro heart, [in] spite of all the maddening influence of oppression is too kind, too full of tenderness and love' to seek vengeance, declared white abolitionist Amos A. Phelps in 1834 [30 *p. 332*]. It followed that white abolitionists must take aggressive action if the slaves were to be freed. Nevertheless, both black and white abolitionists were aware of Nat Turner's revolt, of slave resistance, and the desire of slaves to escape. Most of them assumed, despite racialist theories, that enslaved African Americans had the wherewithal to rise up against their oppressors [102].

A SEARCH FOR COMMON HUMANITY

White abolitionists, in fact, had remarkable empathy for African Americans subjected to slavery and oppression [191]. This empathy had several causes. The Second Great Awakening encouraged the saved to be Christ-like in identifying with and laboring for the poor, the weak, and the oppressed [201]. The new emphasis in northern culture on the sanctity of family life produced an awareness that slavery and the domestic slave trade violated and disrupted black families. Especially when white abolitionists came face to face with the brutality of slavery and its dehumanization of African Americans, they could imagine what it was like to be in bondage. When, for example, William Lloyd Garrison, while living in Baltimore, heard slaves whipped, observed the wounds inflicted, and comforted recaptured fugitive slaves in the city jail, he was able to identify with those 'who are in bonds as bound with them' [38, 115 *p. 237, 218*].

Throughout the antebellum years abolitionists encouraged such emotional bonding with black people in slavery. White abolitionists asked themselves to imagine how they would feel if their wife or daughter were molested by a slaveholder, or if one of their loved ones were ripped away by the domestic slave trade [4(a), 5(a)]. Recalling that Algerian pirates had captured and enslaved white Americans during the 1790s, abolitionists insisted that blacks suffered similarly in the South. In 1846, militant New York abolitionist William L. Chaplin wrote, 'To identify one's self at all hazards and mingle sympathies with the crushed and bleeding victims of proud, imperious despotism ... [is] the crowning act of all virtue' [4(c)].

Garrison set an example for abolitionists in favor of biracialism. During the early 1830s he spoke to black groups, stayed in the homes of African Americans when he traveled, welcomed black abolitionists to his home, and employed black men in publishing the *Liberator*. He opened the newspaper's columns to expressions of black opinion and provided accounts of the activities of black organizations [96, 175].

Under Garrison's leadership, interracial cooperation characterized immediate abolitionism. Unlike earlier white reformers, he recognized that the opinions of African Americans were important. 'Their desire ought to be tenderly regarded,' he wrote in 1832 [96 *p. 57*]. Many white abolitionists believed association with African Americans to be an essential means of breaking down their own prejudices and establishing racial equality through example [87, 121]. 'We must eat, walk, travel, and worship with people of color and show to slaveholders and their abettors at the North, that we will recognize them as brethren', Lewis Tappan told an abolitionist gathering in 1836 [10(d)]. Other white abolitionists were more concerned than Garrison and Tappan that race mixing contributed to the antiabolitionist backlash. But the thrust of abolitionism was toward the destruction of racial barriers.

White abolitionists sought Christian brotherhood and sisterhood with their black colleagues. As the 1830s progressed, they admitted black men to full participation in most antislavery societies and there was considerable interracial socializing. White abolitionists joined African Americans in confronting segregated and inferior schooling for black children. They sought public support for black schools, advocated the desegregation of school systems in the Northeast, and funded black private schools. In Cincinnati during the mid-1830s, white abolitionists of both genders established schools for black children, boarded with black families, and worshiped in black churches [87, 96, 121].

White abolitionists also cooperated with African Americans in resisting segregated seating in northern railroads and stages. They opposed 'Negro pews' in northern churches by inviting African Americans to their own pews. They boycotted segregated churches and established integrated ones [121 *p. 129*]. In 1833, Lydia Maria Child urged whites to 'speak kindly and respectfully of colored people,' to 'repeat to our children such traits as are honorable in their character and history,' and to 'avoid making odious caricatures of negroes' [19 *p. 206*]. The bitter resistance these efforts provoked among nonabolitionist whites testifies to their radicalism.

LIMITS OF BIRACIALISM

Yet, despite their efforts, white abolitionists never overcame their racial and cultural biases. They found it easier to oppose slavery than to embrace the North's impoverished black masses. They tended to associate only with African Americans whom they deemed 'respectable' – those whose social standing approximated their own. Since they regarded white culture to be superior and knew little of black culture, they were stiffly patronizing toward free blacks, not to mention slaves. Often they assumed that black ignorance, indolence, and crime were at the root of white prejudice. They insisted that African Americans could surmount that prejudice only by acquiring literacy, self-control, and proper work habits through following the benevolent example of white reformers [176].

Black abolitionists such as James Forten, Robert Purvis, Samuel E.

Cornish, William Whipper and later Frederick Douglass, Henry Highland Garnet, and Martin R. Delany were 'Christian gentlemen,' who were acceptable socially and intellectually to white abolitionists [232 *p. 197*]. It was these respectable black men whom white abolitionists proposed to integrate into white society and cooperate with in uplifting the more threatening black masses. Lydia Maria Child provided assurances in 1833 that immediatists had 'not the slightest wish to do violence to the distinctions of society by forcing the rude and illiterate into the presence of the learned and reformed.' Frequently Child's own cultural prejudices kept her from perceiving the middle-class orientation of her black associates [232 *p. 197*].

White abolitionists held that the black masses had to improve themselves and shed their inferior culture before they could qualify for equal treatment. 'Till they are equal to other people in knowledge and cultivation, they will not and cannot rank as equals,' declared Garrison during the mid-1830s [87 *pp. 166-7*]. White abolitionists saw themselves as missionaries seeking to free the slaves, promote their spiritual salvation, and uplift them to levels of white civilization. But, the whites' inclination toward romantic racialism made them wonder whether African Americans could succeed [179].

Interracial sex – miscegenation – was an especially awkward issue for abolitionists in a puritanical and racist society. Abolitionists of both races maintained that one's choice of a spouse was a private matter and opposed existing state laws prohibiting interracial marriage. Garrison, for example, initiated a petition campaign that by 1843 resulted in the repeal of Massachusetts's prohibition of such marriages [121, 144, 185, 232]. Such activities, combined with abolitionist commitment to biracialism and equal rights, encouraged claims that they promoted 'amalgamation' of blacks and whites through interracial marriage [5(b)]. Hecklers demanded to know if white male abolitionist speakers allowed their daughters to marry black men.

The perceived threat to white dominance posed by miscegenation contributed to the antiabolitionist riots of the mid-1830s [87]. These riots did not change the abolitionists' intellectual commitment to biracialism. They continued to insist that miscegenation was 'not repugnant to nature' and white abolitionists supported the very few of their black colleagues who had interracial marriages [185 *p. 76*]. But urban violence did encourage white abolitionists to deflect criticism from themselves by pointing out – correctly enough – that slavery rather than abolition was chiefly responsible for interracial sex. They began to maintain that emancipation would bring a decrease in miscegenation rather than an increase.

Slavery, they insisted, had turned the South into a great brothel, in which white masters indulged their sexual passions with defenseless slave women, destroying black families and their own souls in the process. 'At the South,' charged one abolitionist, 'illicit intercourse with the slaves is as common as the shining of the sun' [*35 pp. 279–80*]. Only abolition could save the South and the nation from divine punishment for a sinful debauchery that rivaled that of Sodom and Gomorrah [185].

BLACK ABOLITIONISTS AND RACE

Increasingly, black abolitionists, like their white colleagues, had to come to grips with issues of race. This fell chiefly to a younger generation of African-American leaders, including Henry Highland Garnet, Charles Lenox Remond, Frederick Douglass, Henry Bibb, and William Wells Brown, that emerged during the late 1830s and early 1840s. These representative individuals began their long antislavery careers as public speakers.

Garnet, who had escaped from slavery in Maryland as a small child, delivered his first antislavery speech in 1835 while he was still a student in New Hampshire. A white abolitionist praised the address for its 'beauty' and its 'full, unmitigated, unalleviated and unpardonable blackness' [10(c)]. Licensed as a Presbyterian minister in Troy, New York in 1842, Garnet worked closely with that state's Liberty party, while simultaneously urging African Americans to take the lead in antislavery activism. Referring to white abolitionists, he declared, 'They are our allies – *Ours* is the battle' [*233 p. 134*].

Remond, the son of a successful Massachusetts businessman, became the first paid, full-time black abolitionist speaker when the MASS employed him in 1838. A loyal Garrisonian, he raised money and organized anti-slavery societies throughout New England [104]. In 1840 he served as a delegate to the World Anti-Slavery Convention in London and, like Garrison, protested the exclusion of female delegates by joining them in the gallery. While this opened Remond to criticism from blacks that he had sacrificed their interests for the sake of well-to-do white women, it failed to win him universal support among such women. In 1842, a group of white female abolitionists privately criticized Remond's speaking style as lacking in substance [144].

Douglass, who became the most prominent black abolitionist, escaped from slavery in Maryland in 1838. After hearing Garrison speak in 1841, he – like Remond – began his northern antislavery career as an agent of the MASS. Brilliant and eloquent, Douglass quickly transcended white abolitionist expectations that he would serve as an example of how slavery victimized blacks. 'People won't believe you ever was a slave, Frederick, if you keep on this way,' a white colleague admonished him [*28 p. 116*].

Bibb and Brown, who were fugitive slaves from Kentucky, both began careers as northern abolitionists in 1843. Bibb, who was an associate of Lewis Tappan in the AFASS and AMA, lectured throughout the North during the 1840s. His effort to have Bibles delivered to the slaves of the border South was consistent with the more aggressive northern abolitionism of that decade [102]. Brown, who lectured under the auspices of the AASS in New York and Massachusetts, achieved prominence as the first African-American novelist. His *Clotel; or the President's Daughter*, published in 1853, relied on the Thomas Jefferson–Sally Hemmings affair to explore the issue of miscegenation and its moral consequences [74].

Like other black abolitionists, these four men were well aware that racial prejudice infiltrated all facets of life in the United States. They knew that the antislavery movement was no exception. Even so, black abolitionists were equally conscious that most white abolitionists sought to overcome ingrained racism and were African Americans' loyal allies in the struggle against slavery.

Black abolitionists were less conscious of the fact that they shared many of the cultural biases of their white coadjutors. They often valued fair complexions, generally accepted the superiority of white culture, and assumed that African Americans must emulate whites in religion, morality, education, and industry if they were to succeed in America. They joined white abolitionists in demanding that African Americans become sober, thrifty, punctual, chaste, and diligent in order to achieve white standards of middle-class respectability [121, 185]. In arguing against African colonization in 1852, Douglass defined whites as a 'superior people' and declared, 'We believe that contact with the white race, even under the many unjust and painful restrictions to which we are subjected, does more toward our elevation and improvement, than the mere circumstances of being separated from them could do' [9(c)].

The influence of romantic racialism was evident in the contentions of David Walker, Maria W. Stewart, and Garnet that enslaved black men were too subservient to their masters. 'You are a patient people,' Garnet rhetorically addressed male slaves in 1843. 'You act as though you were made for the special use of these devils. You act as though your daughters were born to pamper the lusts of your masters and overseers. And worse than all, you tamely submit, while your lords tear your wives from your embraces, and defile them before your eyes. In the name of God we ask, are you men?' [*Doc. 11*].

Black abolitionists also found much to praise in white abolitionists. They responded to Garrison's early efforts with affection and loyalty. They supported the *Liberator*, paid for Garrison's tour of England in 1833, and black Bostonians served as his bodyguard. Samuel E. Cornish, who edited the *Colored American*, declared in 1837 that 'the devotion and sacrifices of our white brethren should urge us onward' [7]. A year later Cornish maintained that white abolitionists were the 'wise men of the nation ... the salt of the earth, the leaven which preserves our nation, morally and politically, and which will wipe off American reproach, and eventually be America's glory' [10(e)]. William Whipper praised white abolitionists for checking 'evil dispositions and inculcating moral principles' among African Americans [149 *p. 41*].

Nevertheless the cultural arrogance and racial insensitivity of white abolitionists irritated their black colleagues. By the late 1830s and early 1840s black abolitionists began to speak out against what they considered to be bias within the antislavery movement [87, 144, 221]. Sarah Forten, for example, complained in 1837 that the prejudices of white abolitionists 'obscur[ed] their many virtues and chok[ed] up the avenues to higher and nobler sentiments' [18 *p. 380*].

Other black abolitionists perceived condescension among even the best intentioned of their white associates, who managed to reveal their racial bias even while denying it. Samuel Ringgold Ward observed in 1840 that white abolitionists 'best loved the colored man at a distance' [87 *p. 164*]. In 1860, a white colleague annoyed veteran black abolitionist Robert Purvis by declaring that he 'had eaten with black men, had slept with a black man; and this, perhaps, is as severe a test as man's antislavery character can be put to' [121 *p. 106*].

During the late 1830s black abolitionists objected to what they perceived to be white abolitionist de-emphasis of black freedom while pushing other reforms. Black abolitionists were particularly critical of Garrisonian involvement in women's rights and antisabbatarianism. White Garrisonians were also prone to dwelling on abstractions – such as nonresistance, perfectionism, and disunionism – rather than taking action. Increasingly, too, black abolitionists complained that their white colleagues failed to employ enough blacks in antislavery organizations or in their own businesses [87, 144, 221].

These feelings contributed to a resurgence of black autonomy within the antislavery movement during the 1840s. African Americans revived the Black National Convention movement that had lapsed with the rise of the AASS during the early 1830s. Black men predominated in many of the vigilance associations that were organized to aid fugitive slaves and protect free blacks from kidnappers seeking to sell them into slavery. By the 1850s Garnet and Martin R. Delany had become advocates of black migration to Africa [42, 133, 188].

The best example of dissension between black and white abolitionists is that of Frederick Douglass and the Garrisonians. Douglass had remained a Garrisonian after most black abolitionists had embraced the AFASS and the Liberty party. But a combination of suffocating paternalism among white Garrisonians and Douglass's desire for self-realization led him in 1847 to leave Massachusetts for Rochester, New York where he established his weekly newspaper, the *North Star* [221]. White Garrisonians doubted that

Douglass, who was 'but nine years removed from slavery' [87 *p. 190*], could succeed in this venture. When Julia Griffiths, a white Briton, joined the *North Star* staff as Douglass's assistant, they feared damaging charges of amalgamation would ensue [124].

Garrisonians also charged that Douglass was disloyal in attempting to compete against the *Liberator*. 'I have always feared him,' commented Abigail Kelley Foster [2]. By 1851 Douglass had rejected the Garrisonian proslavery interpretation of the United States Constitution and disunionism. He instead endorsed an antislavery interpretation of the Constitution, the illegality of slavery, and political abolitionism. Throughout the 1850s Douglass and Garrison denounced each other. Garrison suggested that Douglass, as a former slave, could not understand the complexity of the antislavery cause. Douglass classed Garrison with 'the bitterest despisers of the negro race' [144 *p. 89*].

PERSISTENCE OF BIRACIALISM

Such nasty disputes have helped convince some historians that white abolitionist empathy for blacks and engagement in interracial cooperation declined after 1840. But there is considerable evidence that, despite an increase in African-American criticism of white abolitionists, biracialism actually expanded during the two decades prior to the Civil War.

From its initiation, the AFASS engaged black abolitionists more successfully than had the AASS. So did the AMA, which by the late 1840s was the largest abolitionist organization in the United States. Both of these organizations encouraged interracial socialization [62, 121]. Black abolitionists also participated actively in the Liberty party – especially in its radical New York wing – which made repeal of discriminatory state laws a centerpiece of its platform [166]. Nevertheless, several prominent black abolitionists remained loyal Garrisonians. In fact, many of the charges leveled against white abolitionists by black abolitionists are misleading because they were the result of factional disputes between the major abolitionist organizations.

Antislavery societies continued during the early 1840s to pair black and white speakers. White abolitionists continued to lodge black colleagues in their homes. Black abolitionist Frances Watkins Harper, for example, reported from Maine in 1854, 'I have not been in one colored person's home since I left Massachusetts' [116 *p. 104*]. Most significant, as Gerrit Smith's group of radical political abolitionists took more aggressive action against slavery during the 1840s, they cooperated more and more closely with militant African Americans.

Also, although Douglass sought personal autonomy when he broke with the Garrisonians, he was not seeking total independence from white abolitionists. Rather, he left the Garrisonians for Gerrit Smith's faction. Smith subsidized Douglass's *Frederick Douglass' Paper*, two-thirds of whose subscribers were white, and the two men became close friends [9(b), 224]. This was possible because Smith and his white associates had, by the late 1840s and early 1850s, developed considerable empathy with African Americans. 'Gerrit Smith is a colored man,' declared the editor of a black newspaper published in New York City [87 *p. 194*].

Meanwhile black and white abolitionists across the North united in support of the underground railroad and in resistance to the fugitive slave laws. Such increased aggressiveness against slavery and its northern supporters became characteristic of abolitionism during the 1840s and 1850s. It was a development that reflected and enhanced continuing biracialism within the movement.

CHAPTER SIX

A MORE AGGRESSIVE ABOLITIONISM

A major factor in the decision of most abolitionists, regardless of race, to support the AFASS, the AMA, and the Liberty party during the 1840s was that these organizations were more aggressive than the AASS was toward slavery in the South. The great abolitionist postal campaign of the mid-1830s has been portrayed as the peak of northern abolitionist interference in the South [237]. But this is not the case. During the 1840s and 1850s abolitionists became increasingly aggressive in their actions.

Even the AASS initiated efforts aimed directly at the South. Garrison and his associates sought through their new doctrine of no union with slaveholders to weaken slavery by withdrawing northern support for it [102]. The Garrisonians also had ties to Cassius M. Clay, the leading southern abolitionist [213]. In a remarkable example of how nonresistants could be aggressive, Garrison in May 1843 called for slaves to 'declare that it is both your right and duty to wage war against them [slaveholders], and to wade through their blood, if necessary, to secure your own freedom' [10(f)]. But the Garrisonians' contention that the United States Constitution supported slavery, their tendency to stress rhetoric over action, and their disdain for helping slaves escape disenchanted those who wanted to do more than agitate. Most abolitionists believed that Garrisonian tactics, if successful, would only separate northerners from the sin of slaveholding while leaving African Americans in bondage [187].

In contrast to the AASS, the newer antislavery organizations actively promoted abolitionism in the South. Throughout its existence from 1840 until it was replaced by the American Abolition Society in 1855, the AFASS published antislavery propaganda for distribution in slaveholding regions and otherwise encouraged antislavery action in the South. The AMA employed antislavery missionaries in the upper South [102]. Liberty party factions initiated two distinct strategies for weakening slavery on its northern periphery.

THE STRUGGLE AGAINST THE SLAVE POWER

The more aggressive abolitionism of the 1840s and 1850s was in part a product of developments within the antislavery movement. But it also came in response to increasing slave unrest and in the context of a broader struggle between the North and South over slavery and its expansion into the West.

The belief among northerners that southern politicians conspired to use their power within the United States government to extend slavery into new regions dated to the struggle over Missouri Territory's application for admission to the Union as a slaveholding state in 1819. The proposition that a territory located so far north could become a slave state raised a fierce reaction among northerners fearful that their section would be hemmed in by slaveholders and slaves. The crisis ended in 1820 with the passage of the Missouri Compromise that – while admitting Missouri as a slave state and admitting Maine as a free state – prohibited slavery in the rest of the existing United States territories north of the 36° 31′ line of latitude.

While most northerners were satisfied with this settlement, abolitionists during the 1830s further developed the idea that a 'slave power' conspiracy, dedicated to promoting the interests of slaveholders at the expense of non-slaveholders, was a permanent presence within the United States government [101]. During the 1840s this concept transcended abolitionism and became common among northerners. One did not need to sympathize with the enslaved or seek racial justice to believe that a slaveholding aristocracy threatened northern prosperity, westward expansion of free white labor, freedom of speech, press, and petition, and democracy itself [81, 211].

It was the annexation of the Mexican province of Texas to the United States as a slave state in 1845 that led to the proliferation of this outlook in the North [119]. Antipathy to slaveholders intensified as President James K. Polk, a slaveholding Democrat from Tennessee, began in May 1846 a war aimed at securing for the United States an enlarged version of Texas and the huge Mexican provinces of California and New Mexico. As soon as this war against Mexico began, a minority of northern Whig politicians joined abolitionists to denounce it as part of a plot to expand slavery.

Then, in August 1846, northern Whig and Democratic members of Congress united to pass the Wilmot Proviso, which proposed to ban slavery in all territories gained as a result of the war. Although the Proviso never became law, it contributed – along with abolitionist threats to slavery in Washington, DC and other border regions – to a sectional crisis during the late 1840s [162]. By that time, most white southerners were convinced that an abolitionist North aimed to destroy slavery and provoke race war.

The character and outcome of the presidential election of 1848 were especially disturbing to these southerners. That year both major parties had attempted to avoid the issue of the Wilmot Proviso. The Democrats nominated Lewis Cass of Michigan and advocated *popular sovereignty* – having settlers rather than Congress decide the status of slavery in each United States territory. The Whigs nominated slaveholding war hero Zachary Taylor of Louisiana, while remaining silent about slavery in the territories. This evasion led to the organization in the North of the Free Soil party, which opposed slavery expansion. Although most white southerners were relieved when Taylor won the election, they were soon disillusioned. As president, Taylor – who had fallen under the influence of northern Whig leader William H. Seward – insisted on admitting California as a free state without making concessions to the South [47, 153].

Threats by southern leaders to take their states out of the Union unless Congress protected slaveholding interests led to the Compromise of 1850, which temporarily quieted discord between the North and South. The Compromise admitted California as a free state, applied popular sovereignty to New Mexico, and abolished the slave trade but not slavery in the District of Columbia. Most significant for abolitionists was the inclusion in the compromise measures of a new fugitive slave law. It came in response to rising slave escapes and fear among white southerners that abolitionist aid to such escapes was undermining slavery in the border South. The new law authorized federal marshals to assist masters in recapturing escaped slaves, denied jury trials to alleged fugitives, created special federal commissioners to hear cases, and made it a federal crime to help slaves escape [54, 102].

THE ROLE OF SLAVE UNREST

In fact it was enslaved African Americans who encouraged northern abolitionists to be more aggressive against slavery in the South. Nat Turner left an impression among abolitionists that, despite racialist notions of black docility, there were black liberators in the South ready to strike for freedom. A rising number of slave escapes from the border South and two spectacular shipboard slave revolts – on the *Amistad* and the *Creole* – intensified this impression [66, 102]. Abolitionists perceived that slavery was vulnerable on its northern periphery and they developed strategies designed to exploit that vulnerability.

The revolt of enslaved West Africans on the Spanish schooner *Amistad* in 1839 had no direct connection with slavery in the border South. But it did introduce revolt leader Joseph Cinque as a black hero, set a precedent for abolitionist cooperation with slave rebels, and led to the organization of the AMA. Following the Africans' successful revolt, a United States warship captured the *Amistad* and carried the Africans to jail in New Haven, Connecticut [111]. In response, Lewis Tappan initiated legal action that led to a Supreme Court decision freeing them in 1841. The AMA was a product of Tappan's successful effort to return the Africans to their homeland [191].

In contrast to the *Amistad* revolt, the *Creole* uprising in late 1841 *was* a product of slave unrest in the border region. Slavery had been declining in Delaware, Maryland, and northern Virginia for decades as local planters began growing wheat rather than tobacco, as free labor became more plentiful, and as soil fertility declined. During the Revolutionary Era, local planters had also manumitted their excess slaves. But as cotton cultivation spread in the deep South, the planters instead began selling their excess slaves south. This growing domestic slave trade threatened black families and, therefore, encouraged slave escapes. A vicious circle developed as masters during the 1830s and 1840s sold slaves south in anticipation of more escapes [216].

Among the escapees was Madison Washington. He left Virginia in 1840, lived in Canada, and in 1841 returned to Virginia in the hope of rescuing his wife. Instead, Washington was apprehended and shipped with 134 other slaves aboard the *Creole* for delivery to New Orleans's slave markets. While at sea Washington led other slaves in seizing control of the vessel, sailing it to the Bahamas, and gaining freedom under British law for all aboard. Washington, who became a hero among black and white abolitionists, enhanced the impression created by Cinque that slaves were ready to claim their freedom [126]. By 1841 a few northern abolitionists were ready to go south to help them.

THE LIBERTY PARTY

At the same time that abolitionists became more aware of slave unrest, a majority of them embraced third-party politics. The movement for what became the Liberty party began in western New York during the late 1830s. Myron Holley, Alvan Stewart, and other abolitionists in that region were disillusioned with moral suasion and efforts to abolitionize the northern wings of the Whig and Democratic parties. Because Democrats were rarely receptive to their appeals and because northern Whigs claimed to represent Christian morality and antislavery sentiment, most abolitionists had voted for Whig candidates. But as members of a national party, Whig politicians were unable to maintain consistent antislavery positions. They supported slaveholding candidates for the presidency and proslavery measures in Congress [166].

Abolitionists, the Liberty leaders contended, had to save themselves from this sinful complicity in upholding slavery by coming out of the existing parties just as they had come out of proslavery churches [116]. But from the start political abolitionists also had more aggressive intentions. They aimed to transform politics in the North, carry antislavery principles into the South, and change the existing proslavery interpretation of the United States Constitution.

By April 1840, when they nominated James G. Birney – a reformed slaveholder – for president, the New Yorkers had been joined by political abolitionists in Massachusetts led by Joshua Leavitt and Henry B. Stanton. Shortly thereafter they gained the support of Ohio abolitionists led by Gamaliel Bailey and, by 1841, Salmon P. Chase.

Birney had no chance to garner a respectable third-party vote in 1840. This was because northern Whigs presented their presidential nominee, William Henry Harrison, as an antislavery candidate and argued that votes for Birney would help re-elect the incumbent proslavery Democratic president, Martin Van Buren. Out of a total of 2,411,187 popular votes cast, Birney received just 7,056. Birney did better as the Liberty presidential nominee in 1844. After four years of third-party organizing – chiefly in Massachusetts, Ohio, and New York – and a proliferation of Liberty newspapers, Birney received 65,608 votes out of a total of 2,871,906 [166].

This was less improvement than most Liberty abolitionists had hoped for. Angry Whig leaders at the time suggested that Birney was a deciding force in the election. They claimed that his vote in New York came at the expense of Whig candidate Henry Clay and secured that crucial state for the victorious Democratic candidate, James K. Polk. But the Whig charges overestimated Birney's impact, Liberty leaders were disappointed, and that disappointment intensified a debate over third-party aims that had existed since the formation of the party [184, 236].

AIMS OF THE LIBERTY PARTY

All Liberty abolitionists sought to agitate the moral issue of slavery within a political context. They all rejected Garrisonian nonresistance and the contention that the United States Constitution was proslavery. But the dominant Liberty leaders in New York and Ohio disagreed concerning the party's role in destroying slavery, while the Massachusetts faction ineffectively sought a middle course.

The New Yorkers are best described as radical political abolitionists. Led after 1840 by Gerrit Smith and including prominent black abolitionists such as Henry Highland Garnet and (later) Frederick Douglass, they subordinated conventional party politics to their interpretation of God's law and to direct action against slavery in the border South. They insisted that the United States Constitution, interpreted in accordance with the Bible and natural law, made slavery illegal throughout the United States. According to their reasoning, either Congress or the Supreme Court had power to abolish slavery in the southern states [187]. More significantly, they maintained that since all laws recognizing slavery were unconstitutional, it was perfectly legal for slaves to escape and for abolitionists to aid them. As far as the radical political abolitionists were concerned, the most sincere abolitionists were those who dared to go south to put this precept into effect [102].

During the early 1840s, radical political abolitionists Gerrit Smith and Henry Highland Garnet rhetorically called on slaves actively to resist their masters. In January 1842, Smith urged slaves to steal what they needed to escape and urged northern abolitionists to go south to help them [*Doc. 10*]. In August 1843, at a Black National Convention meeting in Buffalo, Garnet advised slaves to stop working in order to force masters either to free them or to initiate a violent confrontation [*Doc. 11*].

In contrast, the Ohio Liberty leaders distinguished between abolitionism as a moral struggle and the Liberty party as a conventional political organization. The party, Bailey and Chase maintained, was bound by the common interpretation of the United States Constitution, which recognized the legality of slavery in the states and the power of Congress over it within the national domain. The proper aims of the Liberty party, said Chase, were to *denationalize* slavery by abolishing it within Congress's jurisdiction, to withdraw all federal support for it within the southern states, and to form abolitionist parties in those states [81]. The Ohio Liberty leaders opposed radical political abolitionist advocacy of United States government action against slavery in the South. They also opposed clandestine efforts to help slaves escape. The Ohioans rejected these tactics because they believed they would reduce the third-party vote in the North and prevent the spread of political abolitionism into the South [102].

Their incompatible views caused continuous strife between the New York and Ohio Liberty organizations. The New Yorkers charged that the Ohio party's Cincinnati leadership wished to free only white northerners from the slave power, claimed that the Cincinnatians disdained African Americans, and that they were callous toward fugitive slaves. Bailey responded that the radical political abolitionists hurt the antislavery cause by advocating illegal acts [101].

The two factions irrevocably separated during the late 1840s as opposition to the expansion of slavery into the territories made the Ohioans' demand for denationalization attractive to a minority of northern Democrats and Whigs. The Barnburner faction of the New York Democratic party as well as the Conscience Whigs of Massachusetts and Ohio had come to oppose slavery expansion and the dominance of slaveholders in the national government. While very few of these Democrats and Whigs were abolitionists, the chance to unite with them in a more powerful antislavery party was irresistible to most Liberty leaders. Therefore, after considerable soul searching, the great majority of Liberty abolitionists joined with them in 1848 to form the Free Soil party [47].

Particularly difficult for Liberty abolitionists to accept were the anti-black sentiments expressed by the Barnburners and the choice of Barnburner leader Martin Van Buren as the Free Soil candidate for president [101]. But only a few joined the radical political abolitionists in flatly refusing to support the Free Soil party. Those few nominated Gerrit Smith for president in 1848 and under a variety of names – including Liberty and Radical Political Abolitionist – maintained for over a decade a minuscule but influential organization centered in western New York [166]. Their more important efforts, however, continued to be devoted to destabilizing slavery in the upper South through aid to the enslaved.

THE UNDERGROUND RAILROAD

This aid took a variety of forms, including assisting individuals who had been kidnapped into slavery, supporting freedom suits initiated by slaves, purchasing freedom, and helping slaves escape. Such undertakings weakened slavery in the border South by challenging the assumption that enslavement was the natural condition of African Americans. Aid to kidnapping victims, freedom suits, and attempts to purchase freedom aroused sympathy among whites and encouraged an antislavery morality. Assisted slave escapes directly undermined the slave system by encouraging panicky masters to sell their chattels south, which – as African Americans sought to protect themselves and their loved ones – in turn produced more purchases of freedom and escapes [215, 216].

All of these forms of direct action against slavery predated radical political abolitionism. They originated among African Americans in the Chesapeake and, as early as the 1790s, attracted local white abolitionist support [136]. But, as the domestic slave trade put more black families at risk of dismemberment, radical political abolitionist doctrines encouraged northerners to go south to aid them [102].

During the early 1840s, when the term 'underground railroad' first appeared in newspapers, abolitionists were divided concerning helping slaves escape. Bailey, Chase, and Cassius M. Clay feared that contacts with slaves undermined efforts to establish abolitionist parties in the South. Some Garrisonians supported helping slaves escape but rarely went South themselves; others deprecated spending scarce funds on 'the running off of slaves' [88 p. 74]. But black and white radical political abolitionists were united in insisting that such direct action would do more to free the slaves than either votes or windy speeches [102, 216].

Underground railroading transcended radical political abolitionism and, even during the 1840s and 1850s, most slaves who escaped did so on their own. There never was a united underground railroad operation with a unified administration [88]. But by the early 1840s there were organized, biracial efforts designed to help slaves escape along predetermined routes from the border South to Canada.

Because going into the border South to help slaves escape required secrecy, the full story of these operations is unknown. Nevertheless, trials of slave rescuers, newspaper accounts, and memoirs reveal three regional underground railroad networks. White students at the Mission Institute in Quincy, Illinois began helping slaves escape from neighboring Missouri during the late 1830s. Three of them – all of whom had ties to the radical political abolitionists – were arrested in 1841. Other men and women helped slaves escape from Kentucky – through Cincinnati, Ripley, and Oberlin, Ohio – to Canada. Former slaves Josiah Henson and John P. Parker each made forays into Kentucky to lead bands of slaves northward along this route [25, 29].

It was, however, a network stretching from Washington and Baltimore northward through Philadelphia, New York City, and Albany to Canada that had the biggest political impact and best illustrates the role of radical political abolitionists. Charles T. Torrey, the editor of the *Albany Patriot* – the radical political abolitionists' leading newspaper – and Thomas Smallwood, a former slave, organized the network in Washington in 1842. Aided by black and white men and women, Torrey and Smallwood helped about four hundred slaves escape. Washington police forced Smallwood to take refuge in Canada in 1843. In 1844 authorities in Baltimore arrested Torrey. He was convicted of helping slaves to escape and was sentenced to serve six years in Maryland Penitentiary, where he died in 1846 [216].

Others took up where Torrey and Smallwood left off. In 1848, William L. Chaplin, Torrey's successor as editor of the *Patriot*, organized a failed attempt by seventy-seven Washington area slaves to escape aboard the schooner *Pearl*. Two years later Washington police arrested Chaplin following a furious gun fight as he attempted to drive a carriage northward from the city with two fugitive slaves aboard. Thereafter Jacob Bigelow, a white northerner, became the chief underground railroad operator in Washington. Bigelow coordinated escapes with William Still, the black Philadelphia vigilant association leader, other black abolitionists, and Lewis Tappan, who by the early 1850s had joined the radical political abolitionists [215].

Today the best remembered underground railroad agent is Harriet Tubman. But, like Bigelow and others who avoided arrest, Tubman was not well known during the 1850s except among a few abolitionists and people she helped. Having herself escaped from slavery in Maryland in 1849, she returned as many as nineteen times to help others. Like Torrey and Smallwood before her, she depended on a network of black and white abolitionists for support [235]. Her bravery and that of other African Americans helped complicate white abolitionist views of black character.

After a Garrisonian suggested that the underground railroad had little antislavery impact because it only went one way, Thomas Wentworth Higginson – a young white abolitionist who knew Tubman – replied, 'Year by year new track is being laid, and the cars are running back again – cars that take these heroic self-emancipated fugitives move heroically back from Canada into the midst of slavery again, that they may bring out their children and their friends with them' [10(h)].

POLITICAL ABOLITIONISTS IN THE BORDER SOUTH

Underground railroading exacerbated long-standing southern white fear of an alliance between northern abolitionists and slaves. This added to the difficulties faced by those who worked openly against slavery in the southern borderlands. Nevertheless, during the 1840s and 1850s, a few native-born southern whites and a few northern transplants promoted political action for either gradual or immediate abolition in Kentucky, Virginia, Maryland, and the District of Columbia. Their activities strengthened the impression among white southerners that slavery was under siege at its northern periphery.

Most of these individuals had ties to the Ohio or New York factions of the Liberty party. But Cassius M. Clay, who became the most famous of the southern abolitionists, had close ties to the Garrisonians as well [213]. Born into a prominent slaveholding Kentucky family, Clay became an abolitionist after hearing Garrison speak at Yale College during the early 1830s. When, a decade later, Clay denounced slaveholders as sinners, rejected the colonization of former slaves in Africa, and established an antislavery news-paper in Lexington, he attracted the admiration of all northern abolitionists [*Doc. 12*]. Garrisonians presented him as proof of the positive impact on the South of their agitation and Ohio Liberty abolitionists sought to convert him from the Whig party [102].

Clay's propensity for ruthless violence and his enlistment to fight in the Mexican War in 1846 diminished northern abolitionist enthusiasm for him. But his daring emancipationist campaign for governor in 1851 and his continued emphasis of Christian morality and black rights restored his reputation. By the mid-1850s he was a leading figure in the radical antislavery wing of the Republican party.

While Clay had ties to all northern antislavery groups, most other southern political abolitionists were identified with just one or two. During the 1840s the tiny Liberty party in western Virginia operated as an adjunct to the Ohio party. By 1848, Clay's Kentucky friend and rival John G. Fee had gained the support of the AMA on behalf of his church-oriented antislavery efforts. In his political efforts, Fee aligned first with the Ohio Liberty abolitionists and by the mid-1850s had become a radical political abolitionist. Fee declared that slavery could never be legal and championed black rights. His associates helped slaves escape [102, 105, 214].

Another southern abolitionist with ties to the radical political abolitionists was John C. Underwood, a former New Yorker who operated about nineteen dairy farms in Virginia's Shenandoah Valley. In 1848, Underwood began employing free labor on those farms as a means of showing its superiority over slavery. He also hoped to attract other northern farmers who might serve as the core of an abolitionist party in Virginia. By the mid-1850s, Underwood, like Clay, had become a Republican. In 1856, slaveholders drove him out of Virginia in response to his public denunciation of slavery for its brutal oppression of African Americans [102].

The political abolitionists' most ambitious southern initiative, however, was the establishment in Washington, DC of the weekly *National Era*, which Bailey edited from 1847 until his death in 1859. A project initiated by the Liberty party and the AFASS, the *National Era* aimed to spread abolitionist sentiment throughout the South [*Doc. 13*]. Meanwhile its office served as the center of an antislavery lobbying effort in Congress.

Although the bulk of the newspaper's large circulation was in the North, it had readers in every southern state, which frightened slavery's supporters as much as its location in Washington. In the wake of the *Pearl* slave escape attempt, proslavery mobs attacked the paper's office three nights in a row and in 1850 southern congressmen established the *Southern Press* in an attempt to counter its influence [101].

Garrisonians and radical political abolitionists denounced Bailey, who successively supported the Liberty, Free Soil, and Republican parties, as only nominally abolitionist. But he retained the respect of local African Americans, who regarded him as one of their more trustworthy white allies in the border South. Neither Bailey nor any of the others who represented northern abolitionist values in the South should be confused with such southern colonizationists as Robert J. Breckinridge and Henry Clay of Kentucky or Hinton R. Helper of North Carolina, whose opposition to slavery was rooted almost exclusively in anti-black prejudice [1, 102].

ANTISLAVERY MISSIONARIES IN THE UPPER SOUTH

To a degree, all abolitionists who labored in the South and subscribed to northern abolitionist concepts of racial justice, were missionaries. But the term best applies to those who attempted to preach an antislavery gospel and/or establish free labor communities in the South.

As early as 1836 David Nelson, a Presbyterian minister from Tennessee who had under Theodore D. Weld's influence become an AASS agent, attempted to make Marion College in Palmyra, Missouri a center of imme-diatism within that slave state. Very quickly a proslavery mob forced him to take refuge in nearby Quincy, Illinois where he established the Mission Institute.

More long-lasting were aggressive religious efforts initiated during the 1840s and 1850s with the support of the AMA and the Wesleyan Methodist Connection. Beginning in 1848, the AMA provided essential assistance to John G. Fee's initiative in Kentucky to circulate antislavery literature among whites and Bibles among slaves, to establish integrated abolitionist churches and schools, and to create an abolitionist community he named Berea [102]. At about the same time, the Wesleyans sent Adam Crooks to preach against slavery in North Carolina. By the early 1850s the AMA had joined in supporting Crooks and his colleagues. The missionaries' job, according to Crooks, was 'to go to the far South, to pronounce that Gospel which proclaims *liberty* to the captive, and the *opening* of the prison to them that are bound' [102 *p. 93*]. The AMA also supported smaller missionary efforts in Washington, DC and Missouri.

Meanwhile there were attempts to establish free-labor colonies in Kentucky and Virginia. In 1854 Delia Webster, a native of Vermont and a former slave rescuer, initiated a long struggle to establish such a colony in northern Kentucky. Although fierce local resistance limited her progress, by 1858 she had enlisted the aid of Lewis Tappan in the venture [159]. A year after Webster began her effort, Fee attempted with some success to establish a similar colony at Berea by attracting northern abolitionists to settle there. In Virginia, efforts of antislavery whites to establish free-labor farms dated to the early 1840s – predating by several years those of John C. Underwood. But such efforts reached a peak in Virginia during the late 1850s as Underwood allied with Eli Thayer, an antislavery entrepreneur from Massachusetts, to launch an ambitious scheme to establish a free-labor colony at Ceredo, in the northwestern portion of the state [102].

THE SOUTHERN REACTION

Slavery's defenders were aware that northern abolitionism had become more aggressive during the 1840s and 1850s. Prior to the Compromise of 1850, their denunciations of abolitionist interference in the border South vied with their objections to the Wilmot Proviso for predominance in their rhetoric. In several instances they portrayed aggressive abolitionism as the more significant of these threats, and they hoped that the new and stronger Fugitive Slave Law of 1850 would serve as a means of stopping abolitionist aid to escaping slaves. When the act proved ineffectual, they became even more fearful that the border South would soon be lost and that abolitionists would then move farther south [102].

Proslavery southerners could do little about abolitionists who remained in the North. But they could counter those brave men and women who ventured into the South to help slaves escape, advocate political abolitionism, establish antislavery churches, or build antislavery communities. Charles T. Torrey was not the only slave rescuer who faced prison and death. Cassius M. Clay and others who advocated abolitionist legislation had their newspaper presses destroyed and faced violence. Proslavery vigilantes repeatedly beat John G. Fee and his associates. There were similar assaults on Crooks and other Wesleyan missionaries in North Carolina and Virginia. Southern law enforcement officials arrested missionaries on charges that they helped slaves escape or incited them to insurrection [102, 105].

Some abolitionists were more aggressive against slavery in the South than were others. But during the 1840s and 1850s virtually all of them were more willing than they had been during the 1830s to find ways of confronting slavery on its own ground. 'What we want, in my judgement, is not resistance to encroachment, but direct aggression,' Chase declared in 1846 [166]. Other abolitionists went beyond Chase's emphasis on formal political organization, and growing numbers of white southerners believed they had to act decisively to counter this abolitionist challenge.

CHAPTER SEVEN

VIOLENT ABOLITIONISM

As abolitionists became more aggressive during the 1840s and 1850s, they grew more violent in word and deed. Increasing numbers of them engaged in antislavery violence and many more openly admired those who used force against slavery. Encouraged by underground railroad efforts and resistance to the fugitive slave laws, such tendencies strengthened bonds between black and white abolitionists. John Brown, the white abolitionist who in late 1859 led a biracial band into the South in a failed effort to spark a slave revolt, represents a culmination of these violent tendencies within American abolitionism.

Abolitionists became more militant within a context of rising violence within the United States that lasted from the 1830s through the Civil War years. There were anti-black and antiabolition riots in several northern cities during the 1830s and early 1840s. The United States Army forced 16,000 Cherokees from their homeland in Georgia to Oklahoma in 1838. The Texas war for independence in 1836 led to the American war against Mexico a decade later. During the 1850s, the struggle between the North and South produced violent confrontations over the new Fugitive Slave Law and the status of slavery in Kansas Territory.

Yet abolitionism did not change from a movement dedicated exclusively to peaceful persuasion to one with no reservations about using force to free the slaves. Despite the official commitment to nonviolence of the AASS and its affiliates during the 1830s, abolitionists often justified slave revolt during that decade. They admired black men who led such revolts and, on occasion, northern abolitionists themselves engaged in defensive violence [102, 121]. During the 1840s and 1850s, as abolitionist endorsement of and engagement in forceful action became common, both black and white abolitionists continued to appeal to nonviolent principles. They were, in other words, ambivalent about violent means throughout the decades prior to the Civil War, although violence became more central to abolitionism as the war approached [87].

NONVIOLENT ABOLITIONISM

As immediate abolitionists organized in the Northeast during the early 1830s, Quaker pacifism, evangelical millennialism, and common sense led them to pledge themselves to nonviolence in the struggle against slavery. The NEASS, organized by Garrison in Boston in 1832, pledged itself to 'peaceful means and to give no countenance to violence or insurrection' among slaves. The New York Anti-Slavery Society, begun by Lewis Tappan in October 1833, declared, 'We have no force but the force of truth' and promised never to 'countenance the oppressed in vindicating their rights by resorting to physical force.' Two months later in Philadelphia the initial meeting of the AASS asserted that Christianity 'forbid the doing of evil that good may come' and called on oppressed African Americans 'to reject the use of all carnal weapons for deliverance from bondage' [121 *pp. 8–9, 20, 23*].

These pledges were sincere and nonviolence remained an important element within the antislavery movement until the Civil War [87]. But circumstances as much as Christian morality shaped the early immediatists' rejection of forceful means against slavery. Not only were memories of Nat Turner's revolt still fresh, violent means were illegal. A small band of abolitionists, already subject to persecution because of its radical views on slavery and race, could not put itself beyond the law or outrage popular opinion by threatening race war in the South. While the AASS anticipated the radical political abolitionists by declaring proslavery laws to be 'before God, utterly null and void,' it also recognized that slavery was legally established in the southern states [121, *Doc. 6*].

Nonviolence among abolitionists developed in conjunction with the feminized masculinity common among evangelical reformers in the North and in reaction to the violence inherent in slavery. Most abolitionists of the 1830s rejected aggressive male behavior in favor of peaceful feminine persuasion [194, 206]. Extremely conscious of the sufferings of slaves, they renounced involvement in systems that rested on force. By 1838 Garrison and his friend Henry C. Wright had organized the Nonresistance Society, which as an adjunct of Garrisonian abolitionism helped split the AASS two years later [121, 145].

In conformity to perfectionist ideas developed by utopian socialist John Humphrey Noyes, nonresistants pledged to disassociate themselves from all violence [175]. They refused to defend themselves and rejected all human governments because such governments invariably rested on force [145]. This Christian anarchism went beyond what most abolitionists were willing to accept in the name of nonviolence. Such close associates of Garrison as Wendell Phillips and Frederick Douglass never became nonresistants, although for years they rejected violent means [126, 174].

Others, such as Lewis Tappan, associated nonresistance with Garrison's heretical religious beliefs and assumed that rejection of human government threatened the northern social order. Nevertheless, Tappan and other evangelical abolitionists approached Garrison in their commitment to peaceful means. They refused to defend themselves and their property or to go to court to seek damages against those who had inflicted physical harm on them. During the 1840s, the AMA reflected this nonviolent commitment by advising its missionaries in the South not to seek legal redress against those who attacked them [121].

THE IMPACT OF SLAVE REBELS

While nonviolence remained an important part of abolitionist reform culture, the specter of slave revolt encouraged black and white northern abolitionists to contradict themselves by condoning antislavery violence. In this manner slaves played a central role in the development of American abolitionism.

From the early 1830s onwards abolitionists warned that, unless masters freed their chattels, the slaves would attempt to liberate themselves violently. A masculine image of a southern black liberator, ready to free his people forcefully, emerged to challenge racialist images among abolitionists that portrayed black men as meek and submissive. 'Slaves are like other men,' Garrison warned white southerners a month before Nat Turner's revolt. A decade later, white Liberty abolitionist Joshua Leavitt contended that it was the slaves' 'GOD-GIVEN' manhood that led to revolts [102 *p. 51*].

Despite an inclination toward feminine values – including nonviolence – abolitionists were very conscious that a broader American culture admired heroic, masculine, and violent struggles for liberty. Both female and male abolitionists recognized that if black men were to claim equal citizenship with white men – women of course could not vote – they must be able to establish their manhood through antislavery violence [217]. Abolitionists also increasingly regarded slavery to be a war of extermination against African Americans [199]. As a result, many of them concluded that Christian morality required a more active response than moral suasion.

Just as important, the violent legacy of the American Revolution and a romantic belief that God raised up heroes to carry out his plan for humanity influenced black and white abolitionists. Like others of their time, they assumed God employed charismatic heroes – such as George Washington – to effect His will [126]. While emphasizing that as a nonresistant he denied 'the right of any men to fight for liberty,' Garrison in 1837 observed that America's revolutionary heritage 'authorize[d]' slaves to 'cut their masters' throats' [27 *vol. 2, pp. 225–8*]. Abolitionists who did not share Garrison's pacifism embraced this revolutionary heritage without qualification. William Jay, a white evangelical from New York, declared that the *Amistad* rebels had committed 'justifiable homicide' because they fought for 'the recovery of personal liberty' [102 *p. 55*].

Abolitionists remained ambivalent concerning the expediency and morality of slave revolt from the 1830s through the 1850s. Regardless of their race, they persisted in questioning the willingness of black men to fight for their freedom. Outright calls for slave revolt remained rare during the former decade. Yet abolitionists recognized a pantheon of black liberators, including Toussaint Louverture, Gabriel, Denmark Vesey, Nat Turner, Joseph Cinque, and Madison Washington [32, 102].

As early as a month after Turner's revolt, the *Liberator* published a fictionalized version of Gabriel's trial that portrayed him as telling his captors that 'we have as good a right to be free from oppression as you had to be free from the tyranny of the king of England' [102 *p. 57*]. In 1841, just after the *Creole* uprising, a Liberty convention on Long Island declared that Madison Washington and his colleagues 'acted in accordance with the principles of the Declaration of Independence ... and we trust their noble example will be imitated by all in similar circumstances' [101 *pp. 59–60*]. 'There are many Madison Washingtons and Nathaniel Turners in the South,' Frederick Douglass told a mostly white audience in 1849, 'who would assert their rights to liberty, if you would take your feet from their necks, and your sympathy and aid from their oppressors' [144 *pp. 236–7*].

DEFENSIVE VIOLENCE

These statements reflect an abolitionist admiration for slave rebels that always qualified their embrace of nonviolence. But the abolitionists' ambivalence concerning means also grew out of their own experience. Northern abolitionists confronted angry mobs during the 1830s and – to a lesser degree – during the 1840s [99, 154]. Those who dared in the upper South to advocate emancipation and racial justice faced physical danger throughout the three decades prior to the Civil War. While some abolitionists stood resolutely by their pacifistic principles, such harrowing experiences led others to reconsider their commitment to nonviolence and contributed to their tolerance of slave violence as well [121].

Determined to protect his business during the New York City riot of 1834, AASS president Arthur Tappan armed his employees with guns. A year later Alvan Stewart and other abolitionists in Utica, New York barricaded Stewart's house and stood ready with muskets against an antiabolitionist mob. Similarly, in 1836, James G. Birney and his sons took up guns to defend their home against rioters who had destroyed Birney's printing press [121]. But it was Elijah P. Lovejoy, the white editor of an abolitionist newspaper in Alton, Illinois, who in defense of his press in 1837 actually opened fire on a mob [*Doc. 9*]. Lovejoy's resort to violence and his death at the hands of the mob forced abolitionists for the first time to confront the discrepancy between their nonviolent rhetoric and a violent reality [63].

A few Garrisonians and Quakers flatly condemned Lovejoy's violation of the AASS's nonviolent pledge. Abigail Kelley, for example, said Lovejoy 'had better have died as did our own Savior saying, "Father, forgive them, they know not what they do."' [121 *p. 42*]. A few others praised Lovejoy as a martyr and predicted that 'emancipation must come through violence.' But most abolitionists wavered just as they did in regard to slave revolt. They simultaneously praised Lovejoy's stand against 'ruffians' and regretted his dying 'with a vile implement of human warfare in his hand' [87 *p. 201*]. The AASS neither condemned Lovejoy's actions nor revised its official opposition to violent means [121].

As antiabolitionist violence declined in the North during the 1840s and 1850s, the most dramatic physical confrontations between white anti-slavery and proslavery forces occurred in the upper South. In some instances abolitionists did not personally resist the mobs of southern whites who attacked them or their property. During the Washington, DC riot that followed the *Pearl* escape attempt of 1848, political abolitionist Gamaliel Bailey told a delegation representing the mob, 'Tell those who sent you hither that my press and my house are undefended – they must do as they see proper. I maintain my rights and make no resistance!' Bailey was able to talk the delegation out of attacking him or his home and the Washington police saved the office of his *National Era* [104 *p. 126*].

In Kentucky and to a lesser degree in North Carolina, however, abolitionists defended themselves or relied on their friends and supporters to do so. Cassius M. Clay of Lexington, Kentucky, like Bailey and most other abolitionists who resided in the South, opposed both slave revolt and assisted slave escapes. But Clay became famous for his dramatic use of violence in defense of himself and other Kentucky abolitionists. Clay, who lost a press to a mob in 1845, used a knife to kill a proslavery opponent in 1849. During the early 1850s, he raised armed bands to defend John G. Fee and other abolitionist missionaries. Moral power, Clay maintained, lost none of its force if backed by '"cold steel and the flashing blade", "the pistol and the Bowie knife"' [214 *p. 19*].

Often, however, the violence employed on behalf of small groups of abolitionists was not enough to protect them in the South. Armed anti-slavery bands were unable in 1851 to prevent Adam Crooks and other abolitionist missionaries from being forcefully expelled from North Carolina. When Fee's association with the radical political abolitionists led Clay to withdraw his protection in 1856, Fee's position in Kentucky became untenable. Proslavery forces drove him and his associates from Kentucky in

1859. It was also in 1859 that similar circumstances led most settlers to leave the free labor settlement of Ceredo in Virginia. The following year Jonathan Worth, the last of the Wesleyan missionaries, left North Carolina after having been jailed for several months [102, 220].

VIOLENCE ON THE UNDERGROUND RAILROAD

Abolitionists sometimes contended that helping slaves escape was a properly peaceful and fundamentally legal antislavery tactic. Garrison said in 1844 that such efforts saved people from bondage 'not ... by any act of violence, but in the spirit of good will to the oppressed, and without injury to the oppressor.' That same year he and a group of black abolitionists asserted that to assist escaping slaves 'instead of being a criminal act, is one that must be pleasing in the sight of God' [102 *p. 79*]. Most of those abolitionists who dared to go into the South to lead slaves to freedom agreed with the radical political abolitionist contention that it was slavery that was illegal under the United States Constitution, not restoring men, women, and children to their natural state of freedom.

But only a minority of abolitionists accepted this interpretation of the Constitution. Nonabolitionists had little doubt that it was against state and federal law to help slaves reach the free states. Every southern state had laws against slave escape and against aiding slaves to escape. The federal fugitive slave laws of 1793 and 1850 empowered masters or their agents to pursue and apprehend escapees in the northern states. Local law enforcement officials often assisted the masters in such efforts. In addition, the 1850 law authorized United States marshals to aid masters, created federal commissioners to hear fugitive slave cases, and made it a federal offense to help fugitive slaves elude recapture [54].

It was also clear, despite Garrison's claims to the contrary, that slave escape frequently involved violence. Fugitive slaves often carried weapons in order to protect themselves from recapture [84]. Abolitionist slave rescuers from Charles T. Torrey, during the early 1840s, to Harriet Tubman, during the 1850s, carried guns and threatened to use them against masters, slavecatchers, and law enforcement officials.

In 1844, Torrey – armed with pistols – threatened slaveholders, a proslavery constable in Gettysburg, Pennsylvania, and black men who served as informers to the Washington city police [216]. Black underground railroad operator John P. Parker contended that there was 'real warfare' in southern Ohio between abolitionists led by John Rankin of Ripley, Ohio and slaveholders from Kentucky. 'I never thought of going uptown without a pistol in my pocket, a knife in my belt, and a blackjack handy,' Parker recalled [29 *pp. 74–5*].

Parker always carried weapons when he ventured into Kentucky to help fugitive slaves. Like Tubman, he sometimes threatened to shoot fugitives whose actions endangered an entire group of escapees. Because of such border warfare along the Mason–Dixon line dividing Maryland and Pennsylvania and along the Ohio River dividing Kentucky and Ohio, slaveholders had good reason to perceive that slavery was under violent abolitionist assault along hundreds of miles of its northern frontier.

RESISTANCE TO THE FUGITIVE SLAVE LAWS

Violent northern abolitionist resistance to the enforcement of the fugitive slave laws was closely associated with underground railroad challenges to slavery. The *Pearl* escape attempt – organized in 1848 by white abolitionist William L. Chaplin – and the August 1850 gun fight between Washington police and two escaping slaves – who were aboard a carriage driven northward by Chaplin – directly influenced the terms of the Fugitive Slave Law of 1850 [21(b)]. This law pushed northward the conflict between escaping slaves and masters that had begun in the borderlands. Abolitionists often aided the escapees and masters enlisted law enforcement officers to help them recapture their bondpeople. The ongoing struggle produced instances of dramatic resistance among northern blacks and whites, abolitionists and nonabolitionists.

There had been longstanding opposition to the earlier fugitive slave law of 1793. From the start, Quaker abolitionists in Baltimore and Philadelphia aided African Americans threatened by the act. Although committed to nonviolent means, these Quakers on occasion confronted armed masters and slavecatchers [168, 188]. According to historian Stanley W. Campbell, 'militant' opposition to the 1793 act rendered it unenforceable in large portions of the North. By the 1840s northern state legislatures attempted to nullify the law within their boundaries by passing 'personal liberty' laws. These laws were designed to protect free African Americans against kidnapping into slavery and to prevent the rendition of fugitive slaves to their alleged masters [54 *pp. 119–20*].

Nevertheless it was African Americans who pioneered violent resistance to the law. As early as 1793 a group of black Bostonians invaded a courtroom, knocked down a constable, and rescued a fugitive slave [39]. Forceful black opposition to the act became common during the 1830s and 1840s [149].

The stronger 1850 law led to more widespread violent resistance and made it increasingly biracial. The act catalyzed into action the pre-existing belief among northern abolitionists that they had a moral duty to use force against the evil of slavery [77, 176]. Abolitionists of both races and all factional affiliations joined with Free Soilers, antislavery Whigs, and (by the mid-1850s) Republicans to defy the new law. Encouraged by Harriet

Beecher Stowe's great novel, *Uncle Tom's Cabin*, which dramatized the plight of fugitives, large segments of northern popular opinion supported forceful resistance to re-enslavement. That resistance in turn shaped a younger generation of white abolitionists that included Thomas Wentworth Higginson, Samuel Gridley Howe, George L. Stearns, and James Redpath [102].

Physical opposition to the law concentrated in New England, western New York, and northeastern Ohio. In large areas of the North masters were able quietly to recover escaped bondpeople. Yet the notoriety of a half-dozen dramatic rescues encouraged white southerners to believe that the North was full of militant abolitionists who favored African-American freedom over the vested interests of slaveholders [54, 176].

In February 1851 – just one month after the law went into effect – a black mob, supported by prominent black and white abolitionists, forcibly rescued a fugitive slave known as *Shadrack* from a Boston courtroom. The following September three African Americans and a slaveholder died in a fierce battle over fugitives who had taken refuge in the Christiana, Pennsylvania home of black underground railroad agent William Parker. In November, a biracial mob led by white abolitionists Gerrit Smith and Samuel Joseph May and black abolitionist Jermain Wesley Loguen, stormed the Syracuse, New York police station to rescue a fugitive known as *Jerry* [54, 167].

Other notable rescue attempts occurred in Boston in 1854 and in Oberlin, Ohio in 1858. In the Boston incident the efforts of black and white abolitionists to rescue Anthony Burns from the local court house failed. But the level of violence – including the killing of one of Burns's guards – forced local authorities to call in state and federal troops. At Oberlin a biracial mob composed of college professors and students, fugitive slaves and other residents rescued John Price from a Wellington, Ohio tavern where he was held pending trial [51, 54].

Although major northern newspapers condemned the abolitionists who engaged in these violently illegal rescues, local popular opinion supported them in nearly every instance. In each case rescuers were indicted and some were jailed. But there were few convictions and none at all in the especially violent Christiana and Anthony Burns cases. In fact, it was their awareness of popular support that encouraged abolitionists to adopt violent means against the Fugitive Slave Law. Prior to the *Jerry* rescue, Gerrit Smith observed, 'It is not unlikely the Commissioner will release Jerry if the examination is suffered to proceed – but the moral effect of such an acquittal will be as nothing [compared] to a bold and forcible rescue. A forcible rescue will demonstrate the strength of public opinion against the possible legality of slavery and this Fugitive Slave Law in particular' [54 *p. 155*].

By the mid-1850s abolitionist resistance had contributed to a climate of opinion that led northern legislatures to pass a new series of 'personal

1. This water colour portrait depicts Elizabeth Freeman when she was in her late sixties, well after her successful freedom suit helped lead to the Massachusetts supreme court decision abolishing slavery in that state.

2. This contemporary woodcut shows a mob attacking the warehouse in Alton, Illinois where abolitionist newspaper editor Elijah P. Lovejoy had stored his printing press. Lovejoy died defending this building.

3. This daguerreotype portrait shows William Lloyd Garrison, the most prominent of the American immediate abolitionists, as he appeared in 1846.

4. This photographic portrait of Frederick Douglass suggests the forceful character that made him the most prominent of the black abolitionists from the early 1840s into the years following the Civil War.

5. This daguerreotype portrait of Lydia Maria Child shows her as she appeared in 1856. A prominent author before she became an abolitionist, Child helped lead the AASS from the early 1830s through the Civil War years.

6. Henry Highland Garnet, a prominent radical political abolitionist, is best known for his militant "Address to the Slaves" in 1843. During the 1850s, he advocated African colonization.

7. Former New York slave, Sojourner Truth became the most prominent black women who spoke publicly in behalf of abolition and women's rights. This photographic portrait shows her as she appeared during the Civil war.

8. A wealthy philanthropist from western New York, Gerrit Smith became an immediate abolitionist in 1835. As the leader of the radical political abolitionists during the 1840s and 1850s, he funded newspapers, underground railroad activities, and John Brown's raid.

liberty laws,' designed to discourage the recapture of slaves and to prevent the kidnapping of free African Americans into slavery [54 *p. 87*]. These state laws, coming as they did amid violent abolitionist obstructionism, gave white southerners more cause to suspect that their interests were not safe in a Union where abolitionists could simultaneously violate federal law and shape northern state law.

THE IMPACT OF KANSAS

Well publicized acts of violent resistance to the new fugitive slave law demonstrated the failure of the Compromise of 1850 to achieve its goal of alleviating southern white fear of abolitionist aggression. Yet as late as 1853 Democratic and Whig leaders hoped to 'crush out' agitation of the slavery issue [101 *p. 160*]. These hopes evaporated following the introduction into Congress of the Kansas–Nebraska bill in January 1854. This legislation further divided the North and South and enhanced the violent tendencies within American abolitionism.

A vision of a railroad stretching from St Louis through Kansas to the Pacific coast motivated Stephen A. Douglas, the Democratic senator from Illinois who wrote the bill. Douglas was a nationalist who despised abolitionists, shared the common assumption that people of African descent were naturally suited for bondage, and believed that slavery had little chance of expanding beyond its existing borders. He hoped that the construction of a transcontinental railroad along a central route would unify the country.

But before the railroad could be built the northern portion of the old Louisiana Purchase had to be organized into territories and Douglas needed southern votes in Congress to pass the Kansas–Nebraska bill that aimed to do this. Therefore he placed a clause in the bill that repealed the Missouri Compromise prohibition of slavery in the region. Under this provision, those who settled the territory would decide by their votes whether or not to allow slavery. While this application of *popular sovereignty* encouraged southern leaders to try to make Kansas a slave state, it outraged a majority of northerners who believed Douglas had sacrificed their interests for the sake of slaveholders [109].

After an extended struggle, the Kansas–Nebraska Act became law in May 1854 and the result was twofold. First, there was a political revolution in the North that produced the Republican party dedicated to stopping the expansion of slavery and removing slaveholders from positions of power within the federal government [92]. Secondly, a violent conflict between anti- and proslavery forces broke out in Kansas. Settlers from the North, who constituted an overwhelming majority in the new territory, battled 'border ruffians' from Missouri and proslavery federal officials. The specter of proslavery aggression in Kansas enhanced the tendency among the great majority of abolitionists to believe that force was required, not only on behalf of fugitive slaves, but against the South itself [203].

Few abolitionists actually went to Kansas Territory. Those who did either went with violent intentions or, after they arrived, quickly gave up their commitment to peaceful means. Charles B. Stearns, a Garrisonian nonresistant prior to his trip to Kansas in 1855, declared, 'These pro-slavery Missourians are demons from the bottomless pit and may be shot with impunity' [145 *p. 241*]. John Henry Kagi, a young correspondent of several abolitionist newspapers, killed a proslavery man during a brawl in 1856 [141].

The most famous of the abolitionists who fought in Kansas was John Brown, who with several of his sons, executed five allegedly proslavery men at Pottawatomie Creek in May 1856 [141]. Closely associated with the radical political abolitionists, Brown had advocated violent action against slaveholders since the late 1840s. His fame as the leading Free State warrior in Kansas allowed him to begin raising funds at abolitionist meetings for a more ambitious assault on slavery in the South itself.

Violence in Kansas also affected the outlook of abolitionists who remained in the East. Gerrit Smith, Wendell Phillips, and other immediatists contributed funds to help antislavery settlers migrate to Kansas and to arm them. Smith declared that 'the shedding of blood [in Kansas] was unavoidable' [87 *p. 206*]. Despite their continuing preference for peaceful means, such women as Lydia Maria Child and Angelina Grimké Weld acknowledged the need for antislavery violence in Kansas [126]. 'We are compelled to choose between two evils, and all that we can do is take the *least*, and baptize liberty in blood, if it must be so,' lamented Weld [87 *p. 206*]. By the late 1850s, those, such as Garrison and Lewis Tappan, who continued to insist on peaceful means perceived themselves to be a distinct minority among abolitionists.

ABOLITIONISTS CALL FOR SLAVE REVOLT

Although abolitionists had expressed admiration for slave rebels since the early days of immediatism, explicit calls for slave revolt – even among black abolitionists – were rare before 1850. Even during the last antebellum decade abolitionists often mixed predictions of slave revolt with denials that they advocated such revolts. For example, Jermain Wesley Loguen, a black radical political abolitionist, pledged in 1850 that black northerners would 'with death-dealing weapons' support slave rebels, while simultaneously denying that he meant to 'encourage, or justify slave violence' [102 *p. 60*].

But by the late 1850s, amid resistance to the new fugitive slave law, civil war in Kansas, and widespread rumors of slave unrest following the national election of 1856, northern abolitionists called forthrightly for a slave uprising. That Garrisonians were prominent among those making such appeals provides conclusive evidence that the long-term abolitionist balance between peaceful and violent means had shifted decisively in favor of the latter. Still claiming to be a nonresistant, Henry C. Wright told the MASS in 1857, 'We owe it as our duty to ourselves and to humanity, to excite every slave to *rebellion* against his master' [102 *p. 61*].

Traditional notions of masculinity – always just beneath the surface among abolitionists – thrived during the violent 1850s. Thomas Wentworth Higginson and Theodore Parker believed it was the duty of white abolitionists to instruct black men in martial valor. Frederick Douglass declared, 'My people can never be elevated till they elevate themselves, by fighting for their freedom, and by the sword obtaining it' [145 *p. 235*].

Violent *rhetoric*, however, was not good enough for John Brown. Emerging from a Garrisonian meeting in 1859, he scoffed, 'Talk! talk! talk! – that will never set the slave free' [34 *p. 131*]. Brown's determination to lead a war for black liberation reflected violent sentiment among abolitionists during the late 1850s. But his outlook was also a product of thirty years of abolitionist admiration for slave rebels and nearly twenty years during which northern abolitionists had gone south to help slaves escape. Brown, as an abolitionist precursor of the Civil War, was as much a product of longstanding aggressive tendencies within the antislavery movement as he was of the sectional conflict of the 1850s.

CHAPTER EIGHT

ABOLITIONISTS AND BLACK FREEDOM

For years historians have noted that it was not the abolitionists who ended slavery in the United States. Rather, it was a combination of Union armies and the actions of the slaves themselves that led to general emancipation following the Civil War. Nor was abolitionism a primary cause of that war or of the sectional conflict between the North and South that preceded it.

Instead, the sectional conflict and the Civil War were products of longstanding, complex, and fundamental cultural, economic, and political forces. As the sectional conflict – which centered on the slavery issue – reached its peak during the 1850s, it transcended the abolitionist movement. The new Republican party, representing a broad array of northern interests, became a bigger threat to slavery than the abolitionists were [66]. But abolitionists were not bystanders as the United States moved toward civil war. Instead, they helped precipitate and shape the war that revolutionized the nation. This is most clear in John Brown's raid on Harpers Ferry, Virginia in 1859, but abolitionists influenced and were influenced by the other defining events of the 1850s.

During the Civil War abolitionists became popular in the North and used their influence to make what had begun as a war to save the Union into a war of liberation. They advocated arming black men as Union soldiers. Younger white abolitionists served as officers in black regiments. Although some abolitionists grew frustrated with President Abraham Lincoln's reluctance to make black freedom a war aim, most accepted his leadership. When emancipation came as a result of the war, they assumed that their years of effort had been vindicated.

THE SECTIONAL CONFLICT DURING THE 1850s

For decades abolitionists had influenced the development of northern popular opinion. Regarded nearly universally as fanatics during the 1830s and 1840s, they nevertheless had much in common with a growing number of antislavery politicians. For example, Congressman Joshua R. Giddings of

Ohio had ties to Garrisonian and Liberty abolitionists, Senator Charles Sumner of Massachusetts was in constant communication with leading Garrisonians, and Senator John P. Hale of New Hampshire was the Liberty party presidential nominee in 1847 [49, 165, 173].

All three of these politicians became Free Soilers in 1848 and their moral opposition to slavery counteracted the racism of others within that organization. By that year as well, the abolitionist concept of a slave power conspiracy was widely accepted in the North. Throughout the 1850s abolitionist defiance of the Fugitive Slave Law brought home antislavery issues to countless northerners. But increasingly during the 1850s, abolitionist attitudes and policies were themselves shaped by the broader sectional conflict.

Civil war in Kansas enhanced violent tendencies among abolitionists. Even more influential was the rise of the Republican party, representing the sectional interests of the North. Between 1854 and 1856 the coalition of Free Soilers and northern Whigs and Democrats opposed to the Kansas–Nebraska Act in particular and slavery expansion in general congealed into this powerful political organization. While the party called for banning slavery in the territories and destroying the slave power in the federal government, it did not during the 1850s, embrace the abolitionist commitment to immediate emancipation and black rights [47, 92]. The idea that it was a 'white man's party' equally opposed to slavery and to African Americans was part of its electoral appeal [188 *p. 265*]. Still, politicians heavily influenced by abolitionism were at its core.

Salmon P. Chase, a Free Soil senator from Ohio and a former Liberty abolitionist who in 1854 helped arouse northern anger against the Kansas–Nebraska Act, became one of the new party's more influential leaders [48]. Another former Liberty abolitionist, Gamaliel Bailey, used the wide circulation of his *National Era* to encourage local Republican organizations across the North. Bailey also helped form the new party by organizing a common congressional caucus among Anti-Nebraska Democrats, Free Soilers, and Whigs [101]. Former Whig William H. Seward, who had in 1850 invoked a 'higher law' against slavery expansion and rivaled Chase for the Republican leadership, frequently communicated with Gerrit Smith and other abolitionists. Throughout the 1850s Chase, Bailey, Seward, Giddings, and others, who became known as *Radical Republicans*, labored to keep the party focused on the slavery issue rather than on ethnic and economic issues favored by conservatives.

Garrisonians and radical political abolitionists recognized that the Republican party had the potential to polarize northern popular opinion against slaveholders [81]. They worked relentlessly to persuade the party's leaders to adopt abolitionist principles. While such efforts had little positive impact on the party's conservative wing, in numerous dialogues abolitionists forced Radical Republicans to show how the party could achieve immediatist goals.

The need of Radical Republicans to work with their conservative colleagues and the differing perspectives of the Garrisonians and the radical political abolitionists weakened the effectiveness of this effort. The Garrisonians, insisting that the Republicans' allegiance to a proslavery United States Constitution corrupted their best intentions, urged them to become disunionists. The radical political abolitionists argued that the Republicans must declare the Constitution to be antislavery and take action against slavery in the southern states as well as in the territories. Both abolitionist groups, nevertheless, united in urging Republicans to purge themselves of racism and become champions of black rights [81, 166].

Meanwhile, dramatic events during the latter half of the 1850s made northerners in general more antislavery. In turn, white southerners grew ever more convinced that abolitionists spoke for the North on issues of slavery and race. Slaveholders were especially conscious that the continuing Kansas controversy was leading nonabolitionist northerners to join militant abolitionists in endorsing the use of force against southern interests [102].

This process quickened when a series of southern assaults on antislavery politicians in Washington culminated in May 1856 with South Carolina Congressman Preston S. Brooks's caning of Republican Senator Charles Sumner. Shortly thereafter several Republican members of Congress armed themselves and dared southerners to challenge them. Soon 'Bleeding Kansas and Bleeding Sumner' became focal points of the 1856 national election campaign.

The three-way presidential contest that year included proslavery northern Democrat James Buchanan, Republican nominee John C. Frémont, and former president Millard Fillmore – the nominee of the anti-immigrant and anti-Roman Catholic American party. While abolitionists were positively inclined toward the Frémont candidacy, most Garrisonians and radical political abolitionists refused to lower their immediatist commitment in order to endorse him. But a few white Garrisonians – including Samuel J. May and Lydia Maria Child – and most black abolitionists – including radical political abolitionists Frederick Douglass and Henry Highland Garnet – became active supporters of the Republican nominee [81, 166]. Meanwhile Democrats portrayed Frémont as an advocate of black freedom and equality. Southern leaders threatened to take their states out of the Union if Frémont were elected, leading slaves in the upper South to believe that Frémont was their champion. When Buchanan won a close contest, rumors of slave unrest spread throughout the region [204].

During the next four years, slaveholders, reacting against what they perceived to be growing abolitionist strength, pursued policies that threatened the North's free-labor institutions. The practical effect was to strengthen the

Republican party and consolidate an increasingly militant disposition among both black and white abolitionists. In a failed effort to force Congress to admit Kansas as a slave state in 1858, in southern rejection of popular sovereignty as a moderate solution to the issue of slavery expansion, and in demands for the re-legalization of the African slave trade, southern leaders risked losing what support they had in the North and incited further abolitionist action.

Of particular significance was the legal case of *Dred Scott v. Sanford*. Scott was a Missouri slave who in 1846 brought suit for his freedom on the grounds that his master had during the 1830s taken him to the free state of Illinois and the free territory of Wisconsin. When – after years of litigation – the Supreme Court ruled in the case in March 1857, Chief Justice Roger B. Taney of Maryland provided a comprehensive opinion that he hoped would resolve the slavery issue in favor of the South. In a seven to two decision against Scott, Taney decreed that African Americans were not United States citizens and 'had no rights which the white man was bound to respect,' that slaves were legally property not people, and that slavery was legal in *all* United States territories [75 p. 347].

Most northerners rejected this decision because it appeared to limit their access to the territories. But abolitionists and their Radical Republican allies emphasized its negative implications for black rights [101]. Gerrit Smith suggested that it would be better to 'hang' Taney than those who might resist the ruling, and black abolitionists were especially angry [100 p. 369]. Charles Lenox Remond urged African Americans to '*defy* the Dred Scott decision' and called on slaves to revolt [149 pp. 231–2]. The biracial Cleveland Disunion Convention of October 1857 resolved, 'It is the duty of the slaves to strike down their tyrant masters by force and arms' [10(g)].

JOHN BROWN'S RAID

It was within this context of growing abolitionist advocacy of violence that on October 16, 1859 a small group of abolitionists led by John Brown seized the federal arsenal at Harpers Ferry, Virginia. Brown's biracial band – consisting of five black and seventeen white men – represented in extreme form the conviction that violence was a legitimate response to an increasingly oppressive racial order. Brown's aim was to lead slaves in a war for freedom [158].

No prominent abolitionists, aside from Brown himself, joined in this brave but seemingly futile assault. Even so, most abolitionists admired Brown's attempt to carry out what they had come to regard as a Christian duty. More than a half-dozen white abolitionists – including Gerrit Smith, Thomas Wentworth Higginson, Theodore Parker, and Wendell Phillips – had helped to finance and plan Brown's mission. Black abolitionists Frederick

Douglass, Jermain Wesley Loguen, and Harriet Tubman all knew about Brown's scheme although they were not all convinced of its practicality [141, 150, 158]

Brown believed that slaves would spontaneously rally to his cause, but there were few slaves or free African Americans in the region near Harpers Ferry. In addition, slaves perceived escape rather than rebellion to be the more practical means of achieving freedom. Within hours local militia surrounded Brown's band. Then United States Marines commanded by Robert E. Lee stormed the building that the raiders had commandeered. Ten of Brown's associates died in the fighting, seven escaped, and the rest – including seriously wounded Brown – were captured, found guilty of treason against Virginia, and executed [66, 141].

Between his capture and his execution the following December, Brown transformed himself from a ruthless man of action into a symbol of antislavery righteousness. He had once surmised that an unsuccessful slave rebel would be able to reshape northern opinion concerning slavery [126]. Now he appropriated that role for himself by giving interviews in his jail cell and writing numerous letters for publication. Like Charles T. Torrey and others who had earlier gone into the South to free slaves, Brown maintained that he had acted in accord with God's law on behalf of 'the millions in this slave country whose rights are disregarded by wicked, cruel, and unjust enactments' [34 *pp. 484–5*]. On his way to the gallows he warned, 'I, John Brown, am now quite *certain* that the crimes of this *guilty land* will never be purged *away* but with *blood*' [*Doc. 16*].

Brown electrified the nation and helped bring on the secession crisis one year later. Convinced that black men must follow Brown's example if African Americans were to gain their freedom, Garrison declared, 'Give me, as a non-resistant, Bunker Hill, and Lexington, and Concord, rather than the cowardice and servility of the southern plantation.' On the day of Brown's execution, Garrison proclaimed, 'Success to every slave insurrection in the South' [87 *p. 211*]. Frederick Douglass, who had refused to join Brown's band, predicted, 'Posterity will owe everlasting thanks to John Brown [because] he has attacked slavery with the weapons precisely-adapted to bring it to the death.' If civil war resulted from Brown's raid, Lydia Maria Child surmised, 'One thing is certain slavery or freedom must die in the struggle' [141 *pp. 315, 319*].

While most Republicans distanced themselves from such sentiment, a few – including Charles Sumner, Benjamin Wade and Salmon P. Chase – had difficulty hiding their admiration. While declaring Brown to be 'rash' and 'criminal,' Chase noted his 'unselfish desire to set free the oppressed' [141 *p. 311*]. Brown had spread abolitionist sentiments among thousands who had previously been indifferent to the slavery issue. On the day he died northern church bells tolled in mourning [130]. Northern poet, essayist, and public speaker Ralph Waldo Emerson, who was not an abolitionist, declared that Brown would 'make the gallows glorious like the cross' [141 *p. 318*].

Among white southerners, Brown enhanced the fear of aggressive northern abolitionism that had been mounting for three decades. The circulation of abolitionist propaganda in the upper South by the AFASS and AMA, abolitionist missionaries, free-labor colonizers, small southern abolitionist political organizations, and underground railroad initiatives all frightened and angered slaveholders [102]. Following the *Pearl* escape attempt, Senator Jefferson Davis of Mississippi had warned that the South had to protect itself against abolitionists 'acting, in fact and in morals, as incendiaries.' It was an issue, he declared, over which Americans 'may shed blood' [21(a)].

Now Brown's raid called forth more fervent assertions of this quite rational white southern resolve. Slave patrols became more vigilant and southern militia readied their weapons [141]. It was after John G. Fee expressed solidarity with Brown's motives, if not his means, that vigilantes drove Fee and his associates from Kentucky [102]. Less justifiably, slavery's defenders assumed that the Republican party supported aggressive abolitionist action to undermine the South's social, political, and racial order. South Carolina's *Charleston Mercury* warned, 'There is no peace for the South in the Union' [54 *p. 120*].

THE CIVIL WAR YEARS

Southern threats to secede from the Union in order to protect slavery from northern interference proliferated as the 1860 presidential election campaign began. The threats became shrill when the break-up of the Democratic party over the issue of slavery in the territories guaranteed a Republican victory. Even though the Republicans passed over antislavery stalwarts Salmon P. Chase and William H. Seward to nominate relatively conservative Abraham Lincoln of Illinois, white southerners quailed at the prospect of a Republican presidency. With good reason, they believed it would mean an increase in underground railroad activity, encouragement of abolitionist political activity in the southern states, and more attempts to instigate slave revolt [102, 176, *Doc. 17*].

Lincoln promised to enforce the Fugitive Slave Law of 1850 and pledged himself not to interfere with slavery in the southern states. He denounced abolitionists. But southern leaders compared him to John Brown. Often deliberately confusing Republicans with abolitionists, white southerners claimed they would not be safe in a Union governed by a Republican president. Consequently, one month after Lincoln's election victory in November 1860, South Carolina began a secession movement that by February 1861 had spread throughout the deep South and led to the establishment of the Confederate States of America. Lincoln's refusal either to compromise on the issue of slavery expansion or to recognize Confederate independence led to the initiation of war at Fort Sumter, South Carolina in April 1861. The secession of the upper South states of North Carolina, Virginia, Tennessee, and Arkansas rapidly followed [81, 102].

The North enjoyed considerable advantages in human and industrial resources as the war began. But a combination of better military leadership, a defensive position, and Union blunders allowed the Confederacy to hold its own during the early years of the war. It was not until July 1863, when the South suffered major defeats at Gettysburg, Pennsylvania and Vicksburg, Mississippi, that Union victory became inevitable. While southern armies slowed the Union advance throughout 1864, superior northern resources overwhelmed the Confederacy during the early months of 1865. The end came in April of that year at Appomattox, Virginia where Robert E. Lee surrendered his Army of Northern Virginia to Union forces commanded by Ulysses S. Grant [129].

Abolitionists almost universally embraced this war as a means of ending slavery. They had never been unqualified pacifists and admired those both black and white who took up arms against slaveholders [87]. The Garrisonians' Christian anarchism and advocacy of disunion to end northern support of slavery did not prevent them from enthusiastically supporting what they often portrayed as a divinely sanctioned crusade. Other abolitionists faced not even these obstacles in endorsing the war effort and they reunited with the Garrisonians in the AASS.

It helped that the war had made abolitionists increasingly popular across much of the North. During the secession winter of 1860–61, a few abolitionist meetings suffered mob attacks as both 'gentlemen of property and standing' and laborers held abolitionists responsible for the crisis [65]. But, generally, northerners honored abolitionists as pioneers in the struggle against the slave power and their numbers and influence increased [66]. 'Never has there been a time when Abolitionists were so much respected,' declared veteran radical political abolitionist William Goodell in December 1861 [15]. As the war progressed, Garrisonian leader Wendell Phillips emerged as the North's most popular public speaker [87].

Well aware of their enhanced popularity, abolitionists worked relentlessly with their Radical Republican allies to convince President Lincoln that the Civil War must be fought not to restore the Union as it existed before secession but to achieve emancipation and racial justice. Abolitionists insisted that the North had a moral obligation to fight for black freedom. They also contended that making emancipation a war aim was sound military policy [128]. 'Not a slave should be left a slave in the returning footprints of the American army gone to put down this slaveholding rebellion,' declared Frederick Douglass in June 1861. 'Sound policy, not less than humanity, demands the instant liberation of every slave in the rebel states' [124 *p. 212*].

Kentucky abolitionist and Radical Republican Cassius M. Clay, who served as Lincoln's ambassador to Russia, told a Washington, DC audience in August 1862, 'As for myself, never so help me God, will I draw a sword to keep the chains on another fellow-being.' Clay, Douglass, and other abolitionists also opposed Lincoln's preference for colonizing former slaves outside the boundaries of the United States. 'As regards the Negro,' said Clay, 'I am opposed to colonization, because it will be a means of delaying emancipation' [102 *p. 171*].

Lincoln refused during 1861 and much of 1862 to heed this abolitionist advice, fearing that fighting for emancipation would alienate the unionist slave states of Maryland, Kentucky, and Missouri and inhibit pro-union sentiment in the Confederacy. It was not until September 1862 that he issued his Preliminary Emancipation Proclamation warning the Confederates that unless they returned to the Union he would declare their slaves to be free. When southern leaders failed to respond, Lincoln, on January 1, 1863, issued his Final Emancipation Proclamation declaring all slaves free in those regions still in rebellion against the United States. Lincoln remained a colonizationist. His proclamations left slavery legal in the loyal slave states and in regions of the Confederacy occupied by Union armies. But he had transformed the war into one for black freedom. As federal forces advanced into regions that had been under Confederate control on January 1, increasing numbers of African Americans became free [129].

However, Lincoln was not responding directly to the urging of Douglass, Clay, Garrison, Phillips, and other abolitionists when he altered his policy in regard to emancipation. Rather, he had come to believe that proclaiming freedom for slaves would aid the Union war effort and that northern popular opinion had shifted in favor of black freedom [66]. It is nevertheless true that a broader abolitionism among Union soldiers and black southerners had forced Lincoln to re-evaluate his policy.

The sort of widespread slave rebellion that white southerners feared, never became a literal reality. But as the Civil War progressed, thousands of African Americans freed themselves by leaving their masters and crossing Union army lines [66]. Their actions raised the issue among occupying Union forces of how to treat ever-growing numbers of black refugees.

In 1861, Union commanders were under orders to return escaping slaves to their masters. But officers found that the escapees were useful as guides, spies, and especially as laborers. The practice, begun that year in Virginia by Union General Benjamin F. Butler, of categorizing the former slaves as 'contraband of war' and refusing to return them to their masters soon spread [130 *p. 266*]. In August 1861 General John C. Frémont went

so far as to issue a proclamation freeing the slaves of Confederate sym-
pathizers in the state of Missouri. Lincoln immediately countermanded
Frémont's decree but he could not countermand the direction the war was
taking.

Meanwhile, Union junior officers and enlisted men, who had marched
to war singing 'John Brown's body lies a-mould'ring in the grave, his soul is
marching on,' became practical abolitionists [55 *p. 556*]. Many of them
were racists and a few committed atrocities against slaves. But more of
them regarded slaves as allies whom they protected against recapture. In
April 1862, for example, soldiers from the 7th New York and 4th
Pennsylvania regiments prevented local constables in the District of
Columbia from seizing a black man accused of being a fugitive slave. Four
hundred soldiers threatened to hang or shoot 'the nigger catchers' [13].

By mid-1862 the enlistment of black troops to fight on behalf of the
Union had become linked with the cause of emancipation. Abolitionists –
especially black abolitionists – led in the advocacy of this policy [*Doc. 18*].
During the late 1850s black vigilance associations in northern cities had
begun to reorganize as militia. When the Civil War began these militia
offered themselves unsuccessfully in response to Lincoln's call for volunteers
[56, 66]. Abolitionists had long contended that black men had to fight for
liberty in order to prove their manhood and establish themselves as citizens.
Now Frederick Douglass asserted, 'Once let the black man get upon his
person the brass letters, U.S.; let him get an eagle on his button, and a
musket on his shoulder and bullets in his pocket, and there is no power on
earth which can deny that he has earned the right of citizenship' [8].

Lincoln, like most whites, doubted that black men could perform
adequately as soldiers. During 1861 and most of 1862 he also feared that
employing black troops – like making emancipation a war aim – could
alienate white Unionists in the South and many white northerners as well.
White Union troops early in the war were disinclined to fight side-by-side
African Americans. But during early 1862 Union generals, usually motivated by pressing manpower needs rather than abolitionism, began enlisting
black soldiers to serve in segregated regiments. At first Lincoln resisted this
tendency, but by January 1863 Union military needs and the logic of black
men fighting in what had become a war for emancipation led him to make
black enlistment a general Union policy. By the end of the war, at least
180,000 black men had served in the Union armed forces [56, 122]. A very
few black women also joined the Union forces. Most prominent among
them was Harriet Tubman, who led a group of black scouts and spies that
was active in South Carolina during 1862 and 1863 [50].

Although abolitionists could not honestly claim to have been solely
responsible for the transformation of the Civil War into a biracial crusade
for emancipation, they had assumed from the war's beginning that it would

become one. By the summer of 1861 the AMA and many smaller abolitionist organizations were sending mostly white but some black missionaries and teachers south to minister to the physical, spiritual, and educational needs of the former slaves. Among the missionaries was John G. Fee who returned to Kentucky to labor among the freedpeople [163]. Other abolitionists played significant roles in the establishment of the Freedmen's Bureau in early 1865 as a government agency devoted to aiding former slaves.

Especially striking was the predominance of women among the abolitionists who went south to help people just emerging from slavery to become wage laborers and citizens. Among them were such veterans in the cause as Maria W. Stewart, Jane Grey Swisshelm, Sojourner Truth, and Margaret Bailey – the widow of Gamaliel Bailey – but most were younger, such as Emily Howland and Josephine Griffing who worked in black refugee camps in the District of Columbia and Virginia. Other young abolitionist women from the North joined with male abolitionists in traveling to South Carolina's sea islands to assist former slaves [126, 135, 150].

Women predominated in such missionary work in part because male abolitionists had joined the Union war effort. Most notably they helped raise and command black troops. With very few exceptions – Martin R. Delany was one – the Union army refused to commission black officers. But such black abolitionists as Frederick Douglass, Henry Highland Garnet, Jermain Wesley Loguen, and William Wells Brown actively recruited black soldiers. White abolitionists William Lloyd Garrison and Wendell Phillips spoke on behalf of black enlistment, and former John Brown confidant George L. Stearns worked full-time finding men to fill African-American regiments, including the famous 54th Massachusetts. Such other white Brown supporters as Thomas Wentworth Higginson and James Montgomery led black troops into battle. So did William Birney – the son of Liberty abolitionist James G. Birney – and Robert Gould Shaw, the young Massachusetts abolitionist who commanded the 54th in its famous failed assault on Fort Wagner near Charleston, South Carolina [56, 95, 124, 126].

Abolitionism during the Civil War, however, suffered from some of the same shortcomings that had always characterized the movement. White abolitionist efforts on behalf of black freedom, in working among the freedpeople, and in raising and leading black Union troops are clear indications of their continuing commitment to racial justice. But, whether they acted under the auspices of the AMA, other northern abolitionist organizations, or the Freedmen's Bureau, most had little comprehension of black culture, sought bureaucratic solutions to human problems, and were paternalistic to the newly freed African Americans whom they increasingly regarded as their clients rather than allies.

Abolitionists accepted that segregated black regiments would be commanded by white officers and generally assumed that whites would serve as ministers and teachers in segregated southern black churches and schools. With some notable exceptions, both black and white abolitionists made similar assumptions in regard to economics. Committed to a wage labor economy, they put too little emphasis on establishing economic independence for the former slaves and expected that the freedpeople would work for whites as wage laborers [122, 128, 202]. When the former slaves did not progress under these circumstances, many abolitionists were disappointed.

A FLAWED VICTORY

In January 1865, four months before the Union victory in the Civil War, Congress passed the Thirteenth Amendment, which abolished slavery throughout the United States. Abolitionists had begun campaigning for the adoption of such an amendment in 1863. William Lloyd Garrison and most abolitionists interpreted its ratification by the states in December 1865 as the successful completion of the immediatist effort they had begun nearly thirty-five years earlier.

Garrison terminated publication of the *Liberator* and urged the AASS and other antislavery organizations to disband. Abolitionists, he recommended, should continue to work on behalf of black rights either individually or in new organizations designed for that task. The Republican party, he believed, could protect African-American interests [128]. But a minority of abolitionists, including Wendell Phillips, Gerrit Smith, Lydia Maria Child, Frederick Douglass, Abigail Kelley Foster, and Robert Purvis, kept the AASS in existence for five more years. Neither group contemplated ceasing work on behalf of the freedpeople [87].

Nevertheless, while the earlier fragmentation of the antislavery movement in 1840 had produced a proliferation of abolitionist activity, this post-emancipation disruption of the AASS signaled the rapid decline of the movement. As early as 1864 abolitionist groups, led respectively by Garrison and Phillips, had disagreed over support for Lincoln's re-election. Garrison and most abolitionists supported the president, but Phillips and an influential minority advocated replacing Lincoln with either Salmon P. Chase or John C. Frémont. In 1866 Garrison supported the Fourteenth Amendment, which provided federal government protection for black rights, while Douglass, Phillips, Gerrit Smith, and others insisted on a more explicit guarantee of black male suffrage [128]. When the Fifteenth Amendment, which included such a specific guarantee, headed toward ratification in 1870, Elizabeth Cady Stanton and other white feminist abolitionists contended that the right of white women to vote was more important than that of black men [98].

For a few years during the late 1860s and early 1870s, as Radical

Republicans influenced federal government policies for reconstructing the country, it appeared that the new constitutional amendments would secure black rights in the South. With the help of the AMA, the Freedmen's Bureau, the Republican party's Union League, and the United States Army, black men briefly exercised citizenship rights in the former Confederate states [82]. But as at least a minority of aging abolitionists understood, both black freedom and these rights had come as a result of northern military victory and Republican political self-interest rather than of a change of heart among white southerners or a commitment among the northern white populace to a biracial society.

In addition, the sort of land reform, government assistance, and continuing military protection that the freedpeople required to establish their economic and political independence was alien to American culture. Even such dedicated abolitionists as Douglass and Phillips subscribed to *laissez-faire* ideas concerning the relationship between government and individuals. Unlike a few abolitionists who continued to labor in the South, most northern abolitionists – both black and white – shared the view that it was up to black southerners to fend for themselves once a narrowly defined legal equality had been established [202].

The result was that abolitionists, divided among themselves once again and hampered by *laissez-faire* precepts, were unable to rally northerners – most of whom had only fleeting sympathy for the freedpeople – in support of renewed intervention in the South when white southerners began stripping away black rights during the 1870s. One by one the southern states established white-supremist governments. They confined African Americans to agricultural labor and deprived them of political rights. By the end of the nineteenth century black southerners faced a system of social, political, economic, and educational segregation designed to keep them in subservience. While conditions were far less bleak for African Americans in the North, even that section fell far short of the immediatist goal of racial equality.

PART THREE   ASSESSMENT

CHAPTER NINE

ABOLITIONISTS AND THE REFORM TRADITION

Nine years after the Civil War ended, when it had become clear that most black people though no longer slaves would remain in subserviency throughout the South, there was an abolitionist reunion in Chicago. Several aging abolitionists who attended lamented that their tactic of peaceful persuasion had been superseded by armed conflict as the means of ending slavery. Violence, they suggested, could not solve the nation's racial dilemma [212]. Historians have tended to agree with this assessment and have used it to help explain the failure of Reconstruction to achieve real equality for African Americans.

But this analysis overlooks two crucial considerations. First, black and white abolitionists had always regarded violence as a possible means of ending slavery. Gabriel, Denmark Vesey, and Nat Turner perceived no alternative to revolt. Northern abolitionists from the mid-1700s onwards acknowledged that an oppressed people might use force to gain freedom. Increasingly, during the antebellum years, they understood that white racial attitudes required that black men fight for liberty in order to claim rights as citizens. By the 1840s abolitionists of both races took the lead in advocating and employing forceful means against slavery. Prior to the Civil War, there were two decades of sporadic fighting between antislavery and proslavery forces all along the border between the North and South as underground railroad agents sought to help slaves escape and southern slavecatchers sought to prevent them from doing so.

Secondly, it was not because slavery died violently that the victory over it was flawed. It was because the United States government's conversion to abolitionism and black rights was based on military and political expediency rather than on a true commitment to racial equality.

In any case, the abolitionists had not achieved their goal of equal rights for black Americans. This is a major consideration in assessing the significance of the abolitionists. Yet this failure should not lead us to lose perspective in evaluating their contribution. We must recall that the same goal eluded Americans during the twentieth century. Also, the abolitionists' inability to convince a majority of whites to accord African Americans equal rights as citizens does not negate their other accomplishments.

During the Revolutionary and Early National eras, black and white abolitionists helped to begin the process of eradicating slavery in the North. During the 1840s and 1850s, they led the way in a partially successful effort to repeal laws discriminating against black people in several of the northern states [166]. Although it was a Union military victory that ended slavery in the South, it was the immediatists' increasingly aggressive tactics that prompted the proslavery strategies that led to war in 1861. Although the sort of black freedom that emerged from the war was flawed, abolitionists had played a major role in destroying legal slavery in the United States.

As biracial activists dedicated to black advancement in America, the abolitionists also pioneered a social and political agenda that directly influenced later civil rights efforts. When black leader W.E.B. Du Bois organized the Niagara Movement in 1905 to agitate for black rights, he specifically recalled the contributions of William Lloyd Garrison and Frederick Douglass [86]. When the Niagara Movement merged into the National Association for the Advancement of Colored People in 1909, former abolitionists and their children were among the new organization's founders. 'In every charge we make against the forces of oppression we have a right to feel that Garrison and Phillips ... are riding at our side', declared the organization's white keynote speaker in 1911 [131 *p. 390*].

Another element in an assessment of the abolitionists' historical role is determining the character of their motivation. In other words, were they radicals or conservatives? In many respects northern abolitionists represented the cultural tendencies of their section's middle class, and historians have, as a result, questioned their radicalism.

In their religious fervor, their free-labor ideology, their devotion to family, their modernizing values, their romanticization of heroic violence, and their disdain for the South and its institutions, they were similar to their nonabolitionist neighbors [185]. Also, white abolitionists never entirely freed themselves of anti-black prejudices intrinsic to the dominant cultures in the North and South. If they exhibited such similarities to other middle-class northerners, how could abolitionists be radicals? Little wonder, from this point of view, that very few historians still regard them to have been irresponsible fanatics.

Instead, as indicated in Chapter One, it is the abolitionists' relevance to the broader sectional conflict that is in dispute. After the failure of the great postal campaign of 1835, several scholars contend, northern abolitionists stopped direct challenges to the existence of slavery in the South. According to this interpretation, they restricted themselves thereafter to convincing a majority of northerners to oppose slavery and favor equal rights for African Americans. Some have gone so far as to maintain that white abolitionists were chiefly concerned with absolving only themselves of the sin of slavery by leaving proslavery churches, proslavery political parties, and – in the case of the Garrisonians – a proslavery Union. Others argue that slavery in the distant South was a largely symbolic issue for northern abolitionists whom they describe as conservatives mainly concerned with establishing a righteous social order in the North [186].

Still, as this book emphasizes, there was much that *was* radical in the abolitionist's reform agenda as well as in their impact on the United States. It is important to recall that abolitionism was never solely a northern white middle-class movement. African Americans played a crucial role in shaping its character. In the South Gabriel, Vesey, and Turner left a legacy of violent black resistance to slavery that made practical abolitionists of countless slaves and free blacks [39].

Their actions created an image of a southern black liberator that shaped northern abolitionism from the late 1820s through the Civil War. Fear of slave revolt was a factor in northern abolitionists adopting a non-violent strategy during the 1830s and paying lipservice to nonviolence throughout the antebellum period. But the admiration of black and white abolitionists for those who violently challenged slaveholders is clear in the writings of David Walker, William Lloyd Garrison, Gerrit Smith, Henry Highland Garnet, Frederick Douglass, and Wendell Phillips, among others. In the North, black abolitionists pressed for action and held their white colleagues to their egalitarian ideals.

The very fact that abolitionism was biracial made it a radical movement. By working and socializing with one another black and white abolitionists challenged fundamental social assumptions. This was evident within northern abolitionist factions, among underground railroad agents, antislavery missionaries in the upper South, and those who resisted the Fugitive Slave Law of 1850. Charles T. Torrey, Harriet Tubman, and dozens of others – both black and white – risked their lives to help slaves escape and to destabilize the slave system on its northern periphery. John G. Fee in Kentucky and his missionary counterparts in North Carolina sought contacts with slaves and created biracial institutions. Those who in the North rescued fugitive slaves from recapture during the 1850s generally acted in interracial groups. John Brown and his biracial band were a product of this abolitionist tradition.

Although political abolitionists in the upper South, such as Cassius M. Clay and Gamaliel Bailey, were less likely to cooperate with African Americans as equals, southern whites perceived them too as threats to their way of life. African Americans in Kentucky had little difficulty in realizing that Clay favored their interests [12(b), 99]. Bailey combined political abolitionism with support for the rights of free blacks in Washington, DC [101]. It is not surprising, therefore, that – after thirty years of increasingly aggressive abolitionism – the election in 1860 of a president who was likely to allow that aggressiveness to expand led southern states to withdraw from the Union to protect slavery and white supremacy.

It is important to recall as well that abolitionism – especially its Garrisonian faction – nurtured feminism and that abolitionist women, led by Lucretia Mott and Elizabeth Cady Stanton, initiated the women's rights movement at Seneca Falls, New York in 1848. By working for equal rights for enslaved African Americans, some middle-class northern white women and some black women of similar status came to recognize their own subserviency to male domination. Patriarchy pervaded antebellum America and women who challenged it faced a daunting task. It was their experience as abolitionists that encouraged them to begin a movement that extends to the present.

Abolitionists also made lasting contributions to American concepts of freedom of speech and press, to constitutional interpretation, to literature, and to popular culture. John Brown, Frederick Douglass, William Lloyd Garrison, Harriet Tubman, and Sojourner Truth remain very much alive as archetypal figures. Truth typifies the strong black woman, plain spoken but eloquent, ready to point Americans in a progressive direction. Tubman is at the center of continuing interest in the underground railroad. Garrison represents the perfect American radical, refusing to compromise moral truth in a struggle against evil. Douglass is regarded as the greatest black leader of the nineteenth century and as one of the nation's more eloquent public speakers.

It is, nevertheless, John Brown, who – at a time when political violence has once again become an issue in the United States – remains most controversial. Growing abolitionist advocacy of and engagement in violent action against slavery foreshadowed the vastly more violent Civil War. Brown epitomizes that violence in the minds of countless Americans. For successive generations he raises the same issue that the abolitionists struggled with themselves: is violent action justified in the pursuit of a good cause?

The American revolutionary tradition maintained that it was justifiable for an oppressed people to rise up against their oppressors and suggested that the friends of the oppressed had a right to assist them. The romantic popular culture that pervaded the North and South in antebellum America celebrated heroic violence on behalf of one's nation, justice, and truth. A people's right to freedom seemed to be tied to the willingness of its men to fight for it. The concept of a law of God that one must be true to in spite of human law, a tradition of vigilante justice, and the broadly recognized right of self-defense all encouraged black and white abolitionists to resort to violent action against slavery and its agents [126]. But can a nation of laws survive when self-appointed groups determine to resist what they perceive to be legalized injustice?

In some instances reform efforts more recent than abolitionism have achieved significant change without resorting to violent means. The women's rights movement has remained largely nonviolent throughout its existence. The Populists of the 1890s, the Progressives of the early decades of the twentieth century, and the New Dealers of the 1930s all achieved significant change at the state and/or national levels through political means with a minimum of violence. But in other cases violence has gone hand-in-hand with reform. During the late 1800s and early 1900s labor unions engaged in bloody strikes to further the legitimate aspirations of working men and women – thereby influencing the Progressives and New Dealers. During the mid-1960s, the previously nonviolent Civil Rights movement turned toward forcible rhetoric and action in a manner similar to that of the abolitionists. Violent tactics have increasingly characterized the religiously-based anti-abortion movement.

The American abolitionists provide us with a way of understanding this interplay of reform, peaceful persuasion, and violent action. Much more important, their history helps us understand the complicated relationships between reformers and the society they aim to change. The abolitionists explored the possibilities for interracial cooperation and racial justice, while demonstrating a limited ability to transcend the very racial biases they challenged. They opposed slavery in part because of the violence it inflicted on African Americans. They advocated peaceful emancipation but they also embraced America's violent heritage. They challenge us to match their commitment, while reminding us that even reformers are bound by the culture of their time.

PART FOUR   DOCUMENTS

John Woolman was one of the more influential Quaker abolitionists of the mid-eighteenth century. While he emphasized that individual slaveholders risked their souls by ignoring God's inner promptings toward human brotherhood, Woolman also warned whites that God's justice could raise oppressed blacks above them.

If we seriously consider, that liberty is the right of innocent men; that the mighty God is a refuge for the oppressed; that in reality we are indebted to them; that they being set free, are still liable to the penalties of our laws, and as likely to have punishment for their crimes as other people: this may answer all our objections [to emancipation]. And to retain them in perpetual servitude, without just cause for it, will produce effects, in the event, more grievous than setting them free would do, when a real love to truth and equity was the motive to it.

...

There is a principle, which is pure, placed in the human mind, which in different places and ages hath had different names; it is, however, pure and proceeds from God. – It is deep, and inward, confined to no forms of religion, nor excluded from any, where the heart stands in perfect sincerity. In whomsoever this takes root, and grows, of what nation soever, they become brethren, in the best sense of the expression. Using ourselves to take ways which appear most easy to us, when inconsistent with that purity which is without beginning, we thereby set up a government of our own, and deny obedience to him, whose service is true liberty.

He that hath a servant, made so wrongfully, and knows it to be so, when he treats him otherwise than a free man, when he reaps the benefit of his labour, without paying him such wages as are reasonably due to free men for the like service, clothes excepted; these things, tho' done in calmness, without any shew of disorder, do yet deprave the mind in like manner, and with as great certainty, as prevailing cold congeals water. These steps taken by masters, and their conduct striking the minds of their children, whilst young, leave less room for that which is good to work upon them. The customs of their parents, their neighbors, and the people with whom they converse, working upon their minds; and they, from thence, conceiving ideas of things, and modes of conduct, the entrance into their hearts becomes, in a great measure, shut up against the gentle movings of uncreated purity.

From one age to another, the gloom grows thicker and darker, till error gets established by general opinion; that whoever attends to perfect goodness, and remains under the melting influence of it, finds a path unknown to many, and sees the necessity to lean upon the arm of divine strength, and dwell alone, or with a few, in the right committing their cause to him, who is a refuge for his people, in all their troubles.

Where, through the agreement of a multitude, some channels of justice are stopped, and men may support their characters as just men, by being just to a party, there is great danger of contracting an alliance with that spirit, which stands in opposition to the God of love, and spreads discord, trouble, and vexation among such who give up to the influence of it.

Negroes are our fellow creatures, and their present condition amongst us requires our serious consideration. We know not the time when those scales, in which mountains are weighed, may turn. The Parent of mankind is gracious: his care is over his smallest creatures; and a multitude of men escape not his notice: And though many of them are trodden down, and despised, yet he remembers them: he seeth their affliction, and looketh upon the spreading increasing exaltation of the oppressor. He turns the channels of power, humbles the most haughty people, and gives deliverance to the oppressed, at such periods as are consistent with his infinite justice and goodness.

John Woolman, [36], pp. 324–7.

DOCUMENT 2   BOSTON SLAVES PETITION FOR FREEDOM, 1773

A committee of Boston slaves submitted this petition to a member of the Massachusetts legislature in April 1773. The slaves demonstrate their familiarity with the natural rights principles on which white Americans resisted British authority. Though the petitioners resort to sarcasm, they are respectful of white authority and moderate in their phrasing.

Boston, April 20th, 1773

Sir, The efforts made by the legislature of this province in their last sessions to free themselves from slavery, gave us, who are in that deplorable state, a high degree of satisfaction. We expect great things from men who have made such a noble stand against the designs of their *fellow-men* to enslave them. We cannot but wish and hope Sir, that you will have the same grand object, we mean civil and religious liberty, in view in your next session. The divine spirit of *freedom*, seems to fire every humane breast on this continent, except such as are bribed to assist in executing the execrable [British] plan.

We are very sensible that it would be highly detrimental to our present masters, if we were allowed to demand all that of *right* belongs to us for past services; this we disclaim. Even the *Spaniards*, who have not those sublime ideas of freedom that English men have, are conscious that they have no right to all the services of their fellow-men, we mean the *Africans*, whom they have purchased with their money; therefore they allow them one day in a week to work for themselves, to enable them to earn money to purchase the residue of their time. ... We do not pretend to dictate to you Sir, or to the Honorable Assembly, of which you are a member. We acknowledge our obligation to you for what you have already done, but as the people of this province seem to be actuated by the principles of equity and justice, we cannot but expect your house will again take our deplorable case into serious consideration, and give us that ample relief which, *as men*, we have a natural right to.

But since the wise and righteous governor of the universe, has permitted our fellow-men to make us slaves, we bow in submission to him, and determine to behave in such a manner as that we can have reason to expect the divine approbation of, and assistance in, our peaceable and lawful attempts to gain our freedom.

We are willing to submit to such regulations and laws, as may be made relative to us, until we leave the province, which we determine to as soon as we can, from our joynt labours procure money to transport ourselves to some part of the Coast of *Africa*, where we propose settlement. We are very desirous that you should have instructions relative to us, from your town, therefore we pray you to communicate this letter to them, and ask this favor for us.

In behalf of our fellow slaves in this province, and by order of their Committee.

Peter Bestes,
Sambo Freeman,
Felix Holbrook,
Chester Joie.
For the Representative of the town of Thompson.

Gary B. Nash, [138], pp. 173–4.

DOCUMENT 3   A BLACK ABOLITIONIST CALLS ON CONGRESS TO TAKE ACTION AGAINST SLAVERY, 1797

Absalom Jones was a founder of Philadelphia's Free African Society during the 1780s and the pastor of one of that city's first black churches. In January 1797 he petitioned Congress on behalf of several African Americans from North Carolina who faced re-enslavement. Although Congress rejected Jones's petition, it is an early example of what became the later radical political abolitionist contention that the national government had power over slavery in the states.

To the President, Senate, and House of Representatives,
The Petition and Representation of the under-named Freemen, respectfully showeth:

That, being of African descent, the late inhabitants and natives of North Carolina, to you only, under God, can we apply with any hope of effect, for redress of our grievances, having been compelled to leave the State wherein we had a right of residence, as freemen liberated under the hand and seal of humane and conscientious masters, the validity of which act of justice in restoring us to our native right of freedom, was confirmed by judgment of the Superior Court of North Carolina. ... yet, not long after this decision, a law of that State was enacted, under which men of cruel disposition, and void of just principle, received countenance and authority in violently seizing, imprisoning, and selling into slavery, such as had been so emancipated; whereby we were reduced to the necessity of separating from some of our nearest and most tender connections, and seeking refuge in such parts of the Union where more regard is paid to the public liberty and common right of man. ...

We beseech your impartial attention to our hard condition, not only with respect to our personal sufferings, as freemen, but as a class of that people who, distinguished by color, are therefore with a degrading partiality, considered by many, even of those in eminent stations, as unentitled to that public justice and protection which is the great objective of Government. ...

If ... we cannot claim the privilege of representation in your councils, yet we trust we may address you as fellow-men, who, under God, the sovereign Ruler of the Universe, are intrusted with the distribution of justice, for the terror of evil-doers, the encouragement of protection of the innocent, not doubting that you are men of liberal minds, susceptible of benevolent feelings and clear conception of rectitude to a catholic extent, who can admit that black people ... have natural affections, social and domestic attachments and sensibilities; and that, therefore, we may hope for a share in your sympathetic attention while we represent that the unconstitutional bondage in which multitudes of our fellows in complexion are held, is to us a subject sorrowfully affecting; for we cannot conceive their condition (more especially those who have been emancipated and tasted the sweets of liberty, and again reduced to slavery by kidnappers and man-stealers) to be less afflicting or deplorable than the situation of citizens of the United States, captured and enslaved through the unrighteous policy prevalent in Algiers ... May we not be allowed to consider this stretch of power, morally and politically, a Governmental defect, if not a direct violation of the declared fundamental principles of the Constitution; and finally, is not some remedy for an evil of such magnitude highly worthy of the deep inquiry and unfeigned zeal of the supreme Legislative body of a free and enlightened people?

Absalom Jones, in [16], pp. 2015–18.

DOCUMENT 4   DAVID WALKER CALLS ON AFRICAN AMERICANS
TO SEEK FREEDOM, 1829

Born free in North Carolina and possibly influenced by Denmark Vesey's antislavery conspiracy in Charleston, South Carolina, David Walker migrated to Boston during the 1820s. In attempting to shape the actions of southern slaves, his Appeal to the Colored Citizens of the World *began a militant tradition among northern black and white abolitionists.*

Are we MEN!! – I ask you, O my brethren! are we MEN? Did our Creator make us to be slaves to dust and ashes like ourselves? Are they [whites] not dying worms as well as us? Have they not to make their appearance before the tribunal of Heaven, to answer for the deeds done in the body, as well as we? Have we any other Master but Jesus Christ alone? Is he not their Master as well as ours? – What right then, have we to obey and call any other Master, but Himself? How we could be so *submissive* to a gang of men, whom we cannot tell whether they are *as good as* ourselves or not, I never could conceive. However, this is shut up with the Lord, and we cannot precisely tell – but I declare, we judge men by their works.

...

When we take a retrospective view of the arts and sciences – the wise legislators – the Pyramids and other magnificent buildings – the turning of the channel of the river Nile, by the sons of Africa or of Ham, among who learning originated, and was carried thence into Greece, where it was improved upon and refined. Then among the Romans, and all over the then enlightened parts of the world, and it has been enlightening the dark and benighted minds of men from then, down to this day. I say, when I view retrospectively, the renown of that once mighty [black] people, the children of our great progenitor [Ham] I am indeed cheered. Yea further, when I view that mighty son of Africa, HANNIBAL, one of the greatest generals of antiquity, who defeated and cut off so many thousands of the white Romans or murderers, and who carried his victorious arms, to the very gate of Rome, and I give it as my candid opinion, that had Carthage been well united and had given him good support, he would have carried that cruel and barbarous city by storm. But they were dis-united, as the coloured people are now, in the United States of America, the reason our natural enemies are enabled to keep their feet on our throats.

Beloved brethren – here let me tell you, and believe it, that the Lord our God, as true as he sits on his throne in heaven, and as true as our Savior died to redeem the world, will give you a Hannibal, and when the Lord shall have raised him up, and given him to you for your possession, O my suffering brethren! remember the divisions and consequent sufferings of

Carthage and of *Hayti*. Read the history particularly of Hayti, and see how they were butchered by the whites, and do you take warning. The person whom God shall give you, give him your support and let him go his length, and behold in him the salvation of your God. God will indeed, deliver you through him from your deplorable and wretched condition under the [white] Christians of America. I charge you this day before my God to lay no obstacle in its way, but let him go.

The whites want slaves, and want us for their slaves, but some of them will curse the day they ever saw us. As true as the sun ever shone in its meridian splendor, my colour will root some of them out of the very face of the earth. They shall have enough of making slaves of, and butchering, and murdering us in the manner which they have. No doubt some may say that I write with a bad spirit, and that I being a black, wish these things to occur. Whether I write with a bad or good spirit, I say if these things do not occur in their proper time, it is because the world in which we live does not exist, and we are deceived with regard to its existence. – It is immaterial however to me, who believe, or who refuse – though I should like to see the whites repent peradventure God may have mercy on them, some however, have gone so far that their cup must be filled.

David Walker, in [17], pp. 79, 82–4.

DOCUMENT 5   **WILLIAM LLOYD GARRISON BEGINS THE *LIBERATOR*, 1831**

The most influential of American abolitionists, William Lloyd Garrison was himself influenced by black abolitionist opposition to gradual emancipation and plans to colonize former slaves in Africa. Although Garrison did not originate immediate abolitionism, he revolutionized the antislavery movement in 1831 by linking that doctrine to equal rights for African Americans.

Assenting to the 'self-evident truth' maintained in the American Declaration of Independence, 'that all men are created equal and endowed by their Creator with certain inalienable rights – among which are life, liberty and the pursuit of happiness,' I shall strenuously contend for the immediate enfranchisement of our slave population. In Park-Street church, on the Fourth of July, 1829, in an address on slavery, I unreflectingly assented to the popular but pernicious doctrine of *gradual* abolition. I seize this opportunity to make a full and unequivocal recantation, and thus publicly to ask pardon of my God, of my country, and of my brethren the poor slaves, for having uttered a sentiment so full of timidity, injustice, and absurdity. ...

I am aware that many object to the severity of my language; but is there not cause for severity? I *will be* as harsh as truth, and as uncompromising as justice. On this subject, I do not wish to think, or speak, or write, with moderation. No! no! Tell a man whose house is on fire to give a moderate alarm; tell him to moderately rescue his wife from the hands of the ravisher; tell the mother to gradually extricate her babe from the fire into which it has fallen; – but urge me not to use moderation in a cause like the present. I am in earnest – I will not equivocate – I will not excuse – I will not retreat a single inch – AND I WILL BE HEARD. The apathy of the people is enough to make every statue leap from its pedestal, and to hasten the resurrection of the dead.

It is pretended, that I am retarding the cause of emancipation by the coarseness of my invective and the precipitancy of my measures. *The charge is not true.* On this question my influence, – humble as it is, – is felt at this moment to a considerable extent, and shall be felt in coming years – not perniciously, but beneficially – not as a curse, but as a blessing; and posterity will bear testimony that I was right. I desire to thank God, that he enables me to disregard 'the fear of man which bringeth a snare,' and to speak his truth in its simplicity and power. ...

William Lloyd Garrison, in the Liberator, January 1, 1831.

DOCUMENT 6   DECLARATION OF SENTIMENTS OF THE
             AMERICAN ANTI-SLAVERY SOCIETY, 1833

The American Anti-Slavery Society, which pledged peacefully to bring about immediate emancipation, without colonization of the former slaves, and without compensation to slaveholders, dominated the antislavery movement during the 1830s. It adopted its Declaration of Sentiments at its initial meeting held in Philadelphia in December 1833.

The Convention assembled in the city of Philadelphia, to organize a National Anti-Slavery Society, promptly seize the opportunity to promulgate the following *Declaration of Sentiments*, as cherished by them in relation to the enslavement of one-sixth portion of the American people.

More than fifty-seven years have elapsed, since a band of patriots convened in this place, to devise measures for the deliverance of this country from a foreign yoke. The corner-stone upon which they found the *Temple of Freedom* was broadly this – : 'that all men are created equal; that they are endowed by their Creator with certain inalienable rights; that among these are life, LIBERTY, and the pursuit of happiness.' At the sound of their trumpet-call, three millions of people rose up as from the sleep of death, and rushed to the strife of blood; deeming it more glorious to die instantly as freemen, than desirable to live one hour as slaves. – They were few in number – poor in resources; but the honest conviction that *Truth, Justice* and *Right* were on their side, made them invincible.

We have met together for the achievement of an enterprise, without which that of our fathers is incomplete, and which, for its magnitude, solemnity, and probable results upon the destiny of the world, as far transcends theirs as truth does physical force.

In purity of motive, in earnestness of zeal, in decision of purpose, in intrepidity of action, in steadfastness of faith, in sincerity of spirit, we would not be inferior to them.

Their principles led them to wage war against their oppressors, and to spill human blood like water, in order to be free. *Ours* forbid the doing of evil that good may come, and lead us to reject, and to entreat the oppressed to reject, the use of all carnal weapons for deliverance from bondage – relying solely upon those which are spiritual, and mighty through God to the pulling down of strongholds.

Their measures were physical resistance – the marshalling in arms – the hostile array – the mortal encounter. *Ours* shall be such only as the opposition of moral purity to moral corruption – the destruction of error by the potency of truth – the overthrow of prejudice by the power of love – and the abolition of slavery by the spirit of repentance.

Their grievances, great as they were, were trifling in comparison with the wrongs and sufferings of those for whom we plead. Our fathers were never slaves – never bought and sold like cattle – never shut out from the light of knowledge and religion – never subjected to the lash of brutal taskmasters.

But those, for whose emancipation we are striving – constituting at the present time at least one-sixth of our countrymen, – are recognized by the laws, and treated by their fellow beings, as marketable commodities – as goods and chattels – as brute beasts; – are plundered daily of the fruits of their toil without redress; – really enjoy no constitutional nor legal protection from licentious and murderous outrages upon their persons; – and are ruthlessly torn asunder – the tender babe from the arms of its frantic mother – the heart-broken wife from her weeping husband – at the caprice or pleasure of irresponsible tyrants; – and, for the crime of having a dark complexion, suffer the pangs of hunger, the infliction of stripes, the ignominy of brutal servitude. They are kept in heathenish darkness by laws expressly enacted to make their instruction a criminal offense.

...

Hence we maintain –

That in view of the civil and religious privileges of this nation, the guilt of its oppression is unequalled by any other on the face of the earth; – and, therefore,

That it is bound to repent instantly, to undo the heavy burdens, and to let the oppressed go free.

We further maintain –

That no man has a right to enslave or imbrute his brother – to hold or acknowledge him, for one moment, as a piece of merchandise – to keep back his hire by fraud – or to brutalize his mind by denying him the means of intellectual, social, and moral improvement.

The right to enjoy liberty is inalienable. To invade it, is to usurp the prerogative of Jehovah. Every man has a right to his own body – to the products of his own labor – to the protection of law – and to the common advantages of society. It is piracy to buy or steal a native African, and subject him to servitude. Surely the sin is as great to enslave an *American* as an *African*.

Therefore we believe and affirm … .

That all those laws which are now in force, admitting the right of slavery, are … before God, utterly null and void; being an audacious usurpation of the Divine prerogative, a daring infringement on the law of nature, a base overthrow of the very foundations of the social compact, a complete extinction of all the relations, endearments, and obligations of mankind, and a presumptuous transgression of all the holy commandments – and that therefore they ought to be instantly abrogated.

We further believe and affirm –

That all persons of color, who possess the qualifications which are demanded of others, ought to be admitted forthwith to the enjoyment of the same privileges, and the exercise of the same prerogatives, as others; and that the paths of preferment, of wealth, and of intelligence, shall be opened as widely to them as to persons of a white complexion.

We maintain that no compensation should be given to the planters emancipating their slaves –

Because it would be a surrender of the great fundamental principle, that man cannot hold property in man.

…

We fully and unanimously recognize the sovereignty of each State, to legislate exclusively on the subject of the slavery which is tolerated within its limits; we concede that Congress, *under the present national compact*, has no right to interfere with any of the slave States, in relation to this momentous subject.

But we maintain that Congress has a right, and is solemnly bound, to suppress the domestic slave trade between the several States, and to abolish slavery in those portions of our territory which the Constitution has placed under its exclusive jurisdiction.

We also maintain that there are, at the present time, the highest obligations resting upon the people of the free States to remove slavery by moral and political action, as prescribed in the Constitution of the United States. They are now living under a pledge of their tremendous physical force, to fasten the galling fetters of tyranny upon the limbs of millions in the Southern States; – they are liable to be called at any moment to suppress a general insurrection of the slaves; – they authorize the slave owner to vote for three-fifths of his slaves as property, and thus enable him to perpetuate his oppression; – they support a standing army at the South for its protection; – and they seize the slave, who has escaped into their territories, and send him back to be tortured by an enraged master or a brutal driver.

This relation to slavery is criminal, and full of danger; *it must be broken up*.

These are our views and principles – these our designs and measures. With entire confidence in the overruling justice of God, we plant ourselves upon the Declaration of our Independence and upon the truths of Divine Revelation, as upon the *everlasting rock*.

...

By the help of Almighty God, we will do all that in us lies, consistently with this Declaration of our principles, to overthrow the most execrable system of slavery that has ever been witnessed upon earth – to deliver our land from its deadliest curse – to wipe out the foulest stain which rests upon our national escutcheon – and to secure to the colored population of the United States all the rights and privileges which belong to them as men, and as Americans – come what may to our persons, our interests, or our reputation – whether we live to witness the triumph of Liberty, Justice and Humanity, or perish untimely as martyrs in this great, benevolent, and holy cause.

American Anti-Slavery Society, in the *Liberator*, December 14, 1833.

DOCUMENT 7	**LYDIA MARIA CHILD ON THE IMPACT OF ABOLITIONISM ON THE SOUTH, 1833**

Lydia Maria Child, a popular writer and close associate of William Lloyd Garrison, was a leading abolitionist of the 1830s and 1840s. A sincere advocate of moral suasion to convince white southerners that they must liberate their slaves for the sake of their souls, she was also aware that northern abolitionists were causing a reaction among slavery's defenders.

The southerners are much in the habit of saying they really wish for emancipation, if it could be effected in safety; but I search in vain for any proof that these assertions are sincere. (When I say this, I speak collectively; there are, no doubt, individual exceptions.)

Instead of profiting by the experience of other nations, the slave owners, as a body, have resolutely shut their eyes against the light, because they preferred darkness. Every change in the laws has rivetted the chain closer and closer upon their victims; every attempt to make the voice of reason and benevolence heard has been overpowered with threatening and abuse. A cautious vigilance against improvement, a keen-eyed jealousy of all freedom of opinion, has characterized their movements. There *can* be no doubt that the *majority* wish to perpetuate slavery. They support it with loud bravado, or insidious sophistry, or pretended regret; but they never abandon the point. Their great desire is to keep the public mind turned in another direction. They are well aware that the ugly edifice is built of rotten timbers, and stands on slippery sands – if the loud voice of public opinion could be made to reverberate through its dreary chambers, the unsightly frame would fall, never to rise again.

Since so many of their own citizens admit that the policy of this system is unsound, and its effects injurious, it is wonderful that they do not begin to destroy the 'costly iniquity' in good earnest. But long continued habit is very powerful; and in the habit of slavery are concentrated the strongest evils of human nature – vanity, pride, love of power, licentiousness, and indolence.

...

When Mr. [William] Wirt, before the Supreme Federal Court, said that slavery was contrary to the laws of nature and of nations, and that the law of South Carolina concerning seizing colored seamen, was unconstitutional, the Governor directed several reproofs at him. In 1825, Mr. [Rufus] King laid on the table of the United States Senate a resolution to appropriate the proceeds of the public lands to the emancipation of slaves, and the removal of free negroes, provided the same could be done under and agreeable to the laws of the respective States. ... Yet kindly and cautiously as this movement was made, the whole South resented it, and Governor [George M.] Troup called to the Legislature and people of Georgia, to 'stand to their arms.' In 1827 the people of Baltimore presented a memorial to Congress, praying that slaves born in the District of Columbia after a given time, specified by law, might become free on arriving at a certain age. A famous member from South Carolina called this an 'impertinent interference, and a violation of the principles of *liberty*!' and the petition was not even *committed*. Another Southern gentleman in Congress objected to the Panama mission because [Simon] Bolivar had proclaimed liberty to the slaves.

Mr. [Robert Y.] Hayne, in his reply to Mr. [Daniel] Webster, says: 'There is a spirit, which, like the father of evil, is constantly walking to and fro about the earth, seeking whom it may devour; it is the spirit of *false philanthropy*. When this is infused into the bosom of a statesman (if one so possessed can be called a statesman) it converts him at once into a visionary enthusiast. Then he indulges in golden dreams of national greatness and prosperity. He discovers that "liberty is power," and not content with vast schemes of improvement at home [in the North], which it would bankrupt the treasury of the world to execute, he flies to foreign lands [including the South] to fulfil "obligations to the human race, by inculcating the principles of civil and religious liberty" &c. This spirit has long been busy with the slaves of the South. ...'

...

If these things evince any real desire to do away with the evil, I cannot discover it. There are many who inherit the misfortune of slavery, and would gladly renounce the miserable birthright if they could; for their sakes, I wish the majority were guided by a better spirit and a wiser policy. But this state of things cannot last. The operations of Divine Providence are hastening the crisis, and move which way we will, it must come in some form or other; if we take warning in time it may come as a blessing. The spirit of philanthropy, which Mr. Hayne calls 'false,' *is* walking to and fro in the earth; and it will not pause, or turn back, till it has fastened the golden band of love and peace around a sinful world. – The sun of knowledge and liberty is already high in the heavens – it is peeping into every dark nook and corner of the earth – and the African cannot be always excluded from its beams.

The advocates of slavery remind me of a comparison I once heard differently applied: Even thus does a dog, unwilling to follow his master's carriage, bite the wheels, in a vain effort to stop its progress.

Lydia Maria Child, [19], pp. 95, 97–8.

DOCUMENT 8   **ANGELINA GRIMKÉ APPEALS TO WHITE WOMEN OF THE SOUTH ON BEHALF OF EMANCIPATION, 1836**

Born into a slaveholding family in South Carolina, Angelina Grimké and her older sister Sarah Grimké moved north to Philadelphia where they became Quakers and abolitionists. In her 'Appeal to the Christian Women of the South,' Angelina refutes biblical defenses of slavery, asks her readers to imagine themselves and their loved ones in the place of slaves, and warns that without emancipation slave rebellions were inevitable.

Some have even said that Jesus Christ did not condemn slavery. To this I reply, that our Holy Redeemer lived and preached among the Jews only. ... That he saw nothing of *perpetual* servitude is certain from the simple declaration made by himself in John viii, 35. 'The servant abideth *not* in the house for ever, the son abideth ever.' If then He did not condemn Jewish *temporary* servitude, this does not prove that he would not have condemned such a monstrous system as that of AMERICAN *slavery*, if that had existed among them. But did not Jesus condemn slavery? Let us examine some of his precepts. '*Whatsoever* ye would that men should do to you, do *ye even so to them*.' Let every slaveholder apply these queries to his own heart; Am *I* willing to be a slave – Am *I* willing to see *my* husband the slave of another – Am *I* willing to see my mother a slave, or my father, my *white* sister, or my *white* brother? If *not*, then in holding others as slaves, I am doing what I would *not* wish to be done to me or any relative I have; and thus have I broken this golden rule which was given *me* to walk by.

But some slaveholders have said, 'we were never in bondage to any man,' and therefore the yoke of bondage would be insufferable to us, but slaves are accustomed to it, their backs are fitted to the burden. Well, I am willing to admit that you who have lived in freedom would find slavery even more oppressive than the poor slave does, but then you may try this question in another form – Am I willing to reduce *my little child* to slavery? You know that *if it is brought up a slave*, it will never know any contrast between freedom and bondage; its back will become fitted to the burden just as the negro child's does – *not by nature* – but by daily, violent pressure. ... It has been justly remarked that '*God never made a slave*,' he made man upright; his back was *not* made to carry burdens as the slave of another, nor his neck to wear a yoke, and the *man* must be crushed within him, before *his* back can be *fitted* to the burden of perpetual slavery; and that his back is *not* fitted to it, is manifest by the insurrections that so often disturb the peace and security of slaveholding countries. Who ever heard of a rebellion of the beasts of the field? ... I appeal to you, my friends, as mothers; Are you willing to enslave *your* children? You start back with horror and indignation at such a question. But why, if slavery is *no wrong* to those upon whom it is imposed?

...

It is manifest to every reflecting mind, that slavery must be abolished; the era in which we live, and the light which is overspreading the whole world on this subject, clearly show that the time cannot be distant when it will be done. Now there are only two ways in which it can be effected, by moral power or physical force, and *it* is for *you* to choose which of these you prefer. Slavery always has, and always will produce insurrections wherever it exists, because it is a violation of the natural order of things, and no human power can much longer perpetuate it. The opposers of abolitionists fully believe this; one of them remarked to me not long since, there is no doubt there will be a most terrible overturning at the south in a few years, such cruelty and wrong, must be visited with Divine vengeance soon. Abolitionists believe, too, that this must inevitably be the case if you do not repent, and they are not willing to leave you to perish without entreating you, to save yourselves from destruction; well may they say with the apostle, 'am I then your enemy because I tell you the truth,' and warn you to flee from impending judgments[?]

Angelina E. Grimké, [24], pp. 13, 24.

DOCUMENT 9   **ELIJAH P. LOVEJOY ADVOCATES DEFENSIVE VIOLENCE, 1837**

The masculine image of slave revolt and the need to defend themselves against the more aggressive of their opponents led abolitionists to advocate and engage in violence. In this excerpt from a letter dated October 3, 1837 – about one month before he was killed – abolitionist journalist Elijah P. Lovejoy explains how antiabolitionist mobs, which had already destroyed two of his presses in Alton and driven him from his mother-in-law's home in nearby St Charles, motivated him and his abolitionist friends to arm themselves.

On our arrival in Alton, as we were going to our house, almost the first person we met in the street, was one of the very individuals who had first broken into the house at St. Charles. Mrs. L[ovejoy] instantly recognized him, and at once became greatly alarmed. There was the more reason for fear, inasmuch as the mob in St. Charles had repeatedly declared their determination to pursue me, and to have my life, and one of them, the fellow from Mississippi, boasted that he was chasing me about, and that he had assisted to destroy my press in Alton. This was the more readily believed, inasmuch as it was known that individuals from St. Louis, where this Mississippian now temporarily resides, were aiding in that work. The mobites from St. Charles also openly boasted here of their assault upon me in that place.

Upon these facts being made known to my friends, they deemed it advisable that our house should be guarded on Monday night. Indeed this was necessary to quiet Mrs. L.'s fears. Though completely exhausted, as may well be supposed, from the scenes of the night before, she could not rest. The mob haunted her excited imagination, causing her continually to start from her moments of fitful slumber, with cries of alarm. ... As soon, however, as our friends, to the number of ten arrived with arms in their hands, her fears subsided, and she sank into a comparatively silent sleep, which continued through most of the night. It is now Tuesday night. I am writing by the bedside of Mrs. L., whose excitement and fears have measurably returned with the darkness. She is constantly starting at every sound, while her mind is full of the horrible scenes through which she has so lately passed. What the final result will be for her I know not, but hope for the best. We have no one with us to-night, except the members of our own family. A loaded musket is standing at my bed-side, while my two brothers, in an adjoining room, have three others, together with pistols, cartridges, &c. And this is the way we live in the city of Alton! I have had inexpressible reluctance to resort to this method of defence. But dear-bought experience has taught me that there is at present no safety for me, and no defence in this place, either in the laws or the protecting aegis of public sentiment. I feel that I do not walk the streets in safety, and every night when I lie down, it is with the deep settled conviction, that there are those near me and around me, who seek my life. I have resisted this conviction as long as I could, but it has been forced upon me. Even were I safe from my enemies in Alton, my proximity to Missouri exposes me to attack from that state. And now that it is known that I am to receive no protection here, the way is open for them to do with me what they please. Accordingly a party of them from St. Louis came up and assisted in destroying my press, the first time. This was well known. They came armed and stationed themselves behind a wall for the purpose of firing upon any one who might attempt to defend the office. Yet who of this city has rebuked this daring outrage on ... citizens of our state and city ... [by] citizens of another state and city? No one. I mean there has been no public expression of opinion on the subject. Our two political papers have been silent, or if speaking at all, have thrown the blame on me rather than on any one else. And if you go through the streets of Alton, or into stores and shops, where you hear one condemning these outrages upon me, you will find five approving them. This is true, both of professor and non-professor [of Christianity]. I have no doubts that four-fifths of the inhabitants of this city are glad that my press has been destroyed by a mob, both once and again. They hate mobs, it is true, but they hate Abolitionists a great deal more.

Joseph C. Lovejoy and Owen Lovejoy, *Memoir of the Rev. Elijah P. Lovejoy* (1838; reprint, Freeport, NY: Books for Libraries, 1970), pp. 251–60.

DOCUMENT 10   GERRIT SMITH CALLS ON SLAVES TO ESCAPE AND ON ABOLITIONISTS TO HELP THEM, 1842

By the early 1840s, slave escapes, shipboard slave revolts, the limited impact of moral suasion on white southerners, and empathy with African-American families disrupted by the domestic slave trade led northern abolitionists to become more aggressive toward the South. Gerrit Smith, the leading radical political abolitionist, provided financial, tactical, and philosophical support to this tendency. As this excerpt indicates, his

'Address to the Slaves in the United States of America,' delivered to a New York antislavery convention in January 1842 reflected a major turning point in the antislavery movement.

AFFLICTED BRETHREN:

The doctrine obtains almost universally, that the friends of the slave have no right to communicate with him – no right to counsel and comfort him. We have ourselves partially at least acquiesced in this time-hallowed delusion: and now, that God has opened our eyes to our great and guilty error, we feel impelled to make public confession of it; to vindicate publicly our duty to be your advisors, comforters and helpers; and to enter upon the discharge of that duty without delay.

Why do abolitionists concede, that their labors for the slave must be expended directly upon his master: and that they are to seek to improve the condition of the one, only through favorable changes wrought in the mind of the other? Is it not because they are not yet entirely disabused of the fallacy that slavery is a legitimate institution? that it has rights? that it creates rights in the slaveholder and destroys rights in the slave? Were they, as they should do, to regard slavery in the light of a sheer usurpation, and none the less such for the hoariness of the abomination; they would have as little respect for the protest of the man-stealer against the direct agency of others upon his stolen property, as they would for the protest of the horse-stealer against a similar liberty with his stolen property. With a vision so clear, they would no more acknowledge a possible acquisition or loss of rights by theft in the one case, than in the other. The same rights, which the slave had, before he 'fell among thieves,' he has now; and amongst them is his right to all the words of consolation, encouragement and advice, we his fellow-men can convey to him.

To make the abolitionist most odious, he is charged with the supposedly heinous and almost matchless offence of communicating with the slave: and the abolitionist, instead of insisting on the right to do so, and instead of publicly lamenting the great difficulties in the way of practicing the right, impliedly disclaims it, by informing his accusers that the abolition doctrine is to address the master and not the slave. No slaveholding sophistry and blustering could obtain such a disclaimer from Paul. That heaven-directed Apostle not only himself communicated with the slave on the subject of his slavery, but directed others to do so. ...

Let abolitionists fully and solemnly utter the doctrine that they are bound to enter into and maintain all practicable communications with the slave; and the candid and intelligent will not only respond to it, but ere they are aware, they will have been carried along by its trains of consequences and influences to the conviction that the abolitionist has a perfect moral right to go into the south, and use his intelligence to promote the escape of ignorant and imbruted slaves from their prison-house. The motto of the abolitionists as well as of our Commonwealth, should be 'HIGHER;' and they should feel, that unless they are continually rising higher and higher in their bold and righteous claims, all past attainments of their cause are left unsure.

...

And now with respect to your own duties. Woeful as is slavery, and desirable as is liberty, we entreat you to endure the former – rather than take a violent and bloody hold of the latter. Such, manifestly was the teaching of Paul to the slaves of his time. What ever was his, the reason for our similar teaching is that recourse to violence and blood-shed for the termination of slavery, is very likely, in the judgment of a large portion of us, to result in the confirmation and protraction of the evil. There are, it is true, some persons in our ranks who are opposed to the taking of human life in any circumstances; and whose doctrine it is, that, however certain might be your success, it would be sinful for you to undertake to fight your way to liberty. But the great majority of abolitionists justify their forefathers' bloody resistance in oppression; and can, therefore, dissuade you from such resistance to a ten thousand-fold greater oppression, not on the high ground of absolute morality, but on the comparatively low one of expediency. ...

Do not infer, from what we have said against violent attempts to recover your freedom that we object to your availing yourselves of any feasible, peaceable mode to accomplish it. We but concur with the great apostle [Paul], when we say: 'If thou mayest be free, use it rather.' Although to run away from slavery is, slaveholders being judges, the most black-hearted ingratitude ... we, nevertheless, call on every slave, who has the reasonable prospect of being able to run away from slavery, to make the experiment.

We rejoice with all our hearts in the rapid multiplication of escapes from the house of bondage. – There are now a thousand a year; a rate more than five times as great as that before the anti-slavery effort. The fugitive need feel little apprehension, after he has entered a free State. Seven years ago, a great majority of the people in the border free States were in favor of replunging into slavery their poor, scarred, emaciated, trembling brother, who had fled from its horrors. But now, under the influence of anti-slavery lessons, nineteen-twentieths of them have come to be ashamed of and to revolt at such monstrous inhumanity. We add, that the fugitive slave may safely continue in some of the free States. ... We leave him, however, to his own free choice, between taking up his abode with us and in the British dominions. If he prefer the latter, we will gladly furnish him with facilities for realizing his preference. The abolitionist knows no more grateful employment than that of carrying the dog and rifle-hunted slave to Canada.

···

We shall get as many copies of this Address, as we can into the hands of your white friends in the slave States. To these, as also to the few (alas how few!) of the colored people of the South, who, some by permission and some by stealth, have obtained the art of reading, we look to acquaint you with its contents. Communications of similar design – that of enlightening and comforting you – will probably be made from time to time hereafter.

···

The principles of abolition have already struck their roots deep in the genial soil of the free States of our Union; and even at the South, abolitionists are multiplying rapidly. ...

Wounded, writhing slavery still cries, 'let me alone – let me alone.' But the people will not let it alone: and such providences, as the insurrections on board of the Amistad and the Creole, show that God will not let it alone. His decree has gone forth, that slavery shall continue to be tortured, even unto death. 'Lift up your heads,' then brethren, 'for your redemption draweth nigh.'

Gerrit Smith, in the *Liberator,* February 11, 1842.

DOCUMENT 11   HENRY HIGHLAND GARNET CALLS ON SLAVES TO CHALLENGE THEIR MASTERS, 1843

Black abolitionist Henry Highland Garnet took the new abolitionist aggressiveness toward the South a step beyond Gerrit Smith's 'Address to the Slaves.' Garnet delivered his 'Address to the Slaves' on August 16, 1843 before a black national convention meeting in Buffalo. Garnet, who was an ally of Smith and clearly influenced by David Walker, suggested hesitantly – but more explicitly than Smith had – that slaves might use violence in seeking liberation. The convention narrowly rejected the address. It was, nevertheless, another sign of growing militancy among abolitionists and especially black abolitionists.

BRETHREN AND FELLOW CITIZENS:

Your brethren of the north, east, and west have been accustomed to meet together in National Conventions, to sympathize with each other, and to weep over your unhappy condition. In these meetings we have addressed all classes of the free, but we have never until this time, sent a word of consolation and advice to you. We have been contented in sitting still and mourning over your sorrows, earnestly hoping that before this day, your sacred Liberties would have been restored. But, we have hoped in vain. Years have rolled on, and tens of thousands have been borne on streams of blood, and tears, to the shores of eternity. While you have been oppressed, we have also been partakers with you; nor can we be free while you are enslaved. We therefore write to you as being bound with you.

Many of you are bound to us, not only by the ties of common humanity, but we are connected by the more tender relations of parents, wives, husbands, children, brothers, and sisters, and friends. As such we most affectionately address you.

...

SLAVERY! How much misery is comprehended in that single word. What mind is there that does not shrink from its direful effects? Unless the image of God is obliterated from the soul, all men cherish the love of Liberty. The nice discerning political economist does not regard the sacred right, more than the untutored African who roams in the wilds of Congo. Nor has the one more right to the full enjoyment of his freedom than the other. In every man's mind the good seeds of Liberty are planted, and he who brings his fellow down so low, as to make him contented with a condition of slavery, commits the highest crime against God and man. Brethren, your oppressors aim to do this. They endeavor to make you as much like brutes as possible. When they have blinded the eyes of your mind – when they have embittered the sweet waters of life – when they have shut out the light which shines from the word of God – then, and not till then has American slavery done its perfect work.

TO SUCH DEGRADATION IT IS SINFUL IN THE EXTREME FOR YOU TO MAKE VOLUNTARY SUBMISSION. The divine commandments, you are duty bound to reverence, and obey. If you do not obey them you will surely meet with the displeasure of the Almighty. ... NEITHER GOD, NOR ANGELS, OR JUST MEN COMMAND YOU TO SUFFER FOR A SINGLE MOMENT. THEREFORE IT IS YOUR SOLEMN AND IMPERATIVE DUTY TO USE EVERY MEANS, BOTH MORAL, INTELLECTUAL, AND PHYSICAL, THAT PROMISE SUCCESS.

...

Brethren, the time has come when you must act for yourselves. It is an old and true saying that 'if hereditary bondsmen would be free, they must themselves strike the blow.' You can plead your own cause, and do the work of emancipation better than any other. ... Go to your lordly enslavers, and tell them plainly, that YOU ARE DETERMINED TO BE FREE. Appeal to their sense of justice, and tell them that they have no more right to oppress you, than you have to enslave them. Entreat them to remove the grievous burdens which they have imposed upon you, and to remunerate you for your labor. Promise them renewed diligence in the cultivation of the soil, if they will render to you an equivalent for your services. ... Do this, and forever after cease to toil for the heartless tyrants, who give you no other reward but stripes and abuse. If they then commence the work of death, they, and not you, will be responsible for the consequences. You had far better all die – *die immediately*, than live like slaves, and entail your wretchedness upon your posterity. If you would be free in this generation, here is your only hope. However much you and all of us may desire it, there is not much hope of Redemption without the shedding of blood. If you must bleed, let it all come at once – rather, *die freemen, than live to be slaves.*

...

We do not advise you to attempt a revolution with the sword, because it would be INEXPEDIENT. Your numbers are too small, and moreover the rising spirit of the age, and the spirit of the gospel, are opposed to war and bloodshed. But from this moment cease to labor for tyrants who will not remunerate you. Let every slave throughout the land do this, and the days of slavery are numbered. You cannot be more oppressed than you have been – you cannot suffer greater cruelties than you have already. RATHER DIE FREEMEN, THAN LIVE TO BE SLAVES. Remember that you are THREE MILLIONS.

It is in your power so to torment the God-cursed slaveholders, that they will be glad to let you go free. If the scale was turned and black men were the masters, and white men the slaves, every destructive agent and element would be employed to lay the oppressor low. ... But you are a patient people. You act as though your daughters were born to pamper the lusts of your masters and overseers. And worse than all, you tamely submit, while your lords tear your wives from your embraces, and defile them before your eyes. In the name of God we ask, are you men? Where is the blood of your fathers? Has it all run out of your veins? Awake, awake; millions of voices are calling you! Your dead fathers speak to you from their graves. Heaven, as with a voice of thunder, calls on you to arise from the dust.

Let your motto be RESISTANCE! RESISTANCE! RESISTANCE! No oppressed people have ever secured their Liberty without resistance. ...

Henry Highland Garnet, in [32], vol. 3, 403–11.

DOCUMENT 12   **CASSIUS M. CLAY ON THE SINFULNESS OF SLAVERY, 1845**

Cassius M. Clay of Kentucky was the best known of the white southern abolitionists. An advocate and practitioner of defensive violence, a gradualist, and a politician, Clay has often been used by historians as an example of the differences between northern and southern abolitionism. He has been unjustly portrayed as a racist who opposed slavery only because he believed the institution harmed nonslaveholding whites. This excerpt from Clay's 'Appeal to All the Followers of Christ in the American Union,' published in his True American *in December 1845, though relatively moderate, is similar to northern abolitionism in its moral stand against slavery.*

To all the adherents of the Christian religion, Catholic and Protestant, in the American Union, the writer of this article would respectfully represent, that he is but a single individual of humble pretensions struggling with honest zeal for the liberties of his country and the common rights of mankind. He sets up no claims to piety or purity of life; but whilst he is himself subject to all the infirmities of our common nature, he believes in an omnipotent and benevolent God over-ruling the universe by fixed and eternal laws. He believes that man's greatest happiness consists in a wise understanding and a strict observance of all the laws of his being, moral, mental, and physical; which are best set forth in the Christian code of ethics. He believes that the Christian religion is the truest basis of justice, mercy, truth, and happiness known among men. As a politician especially, does he regard Christian morality as the basis of national and constitutional *liberty*. He believes that there is now a crisis in the affairs of our nation, which calls for the united efforts of all good men to save us from dishonor and ruin.

Slavery is our great national sin, and must be destroyed, or we are lost. From a small cloud, not larger than a man's hand, it has overspread the whole heavens. Three millions of our fellow men, all children of the same Father, are held in absolute servitude, and the most unqualified despotism. By a strange oversight, or self-avenging criminality of our fathers, an anti-republican, unequal, sham representation has given the slaveocracy a concentrated power which subjects the additional fifteen million of whites of this nation to the caprice and rule of some *three hundred and fifty thousand slaveholders*. They monopolize the principal offices of honor and profit, control our foreign relations, and internal policy of economical progress. They have forced us into unjust wars – national bad faith – and large and unnecessary expenditures of money. They have violated time after time, the national and state constitutions. They have trampled under foot all of the cardinal principles of our inherited liberty. ... They have murdered our citizens – imprisoned our seamen – and denied us all redress in the courts of national judicature. ... All this we have borne, in magnanimous forbearance, or tame subserviency; till remonstrance is regarded as criminal; and it has become the common law of the land, in all the states to murder in cold blood, and in a calm and 'dignified manner,' any American freeman, who has the spirit to exercise the constitutional and natural, and inalienable rights of free thought and manly utterance!

Now, in the name of that religion which teaches us to love our neighbor as ourself – to do unto others as we would have others should do unto us – to break every yoke, and let the oppressed go free – we pray every follower of Christ to bear testimony against this crime against man and God: which fills our souls with cruelty and crime – stains our hands with blood – and overthrows every principle of national and constitutional liberty, for which the good and great souled patriots of all ages laid down their lives, and for which our fathers suffered bled, and died.

...

We know that in 1776 the prayers of the Church, went up from the closet, the altar, and from the field of battle to the Great Arbiter of the destinies of war; we believe that a time of equal danger and awful responsibility is at hand; and we now ask that the prayers of the universal Church be uttered in the cause of liberty once more.

Cassius M. Clay, [20], pp. 358–9.

DOCUMENT 13   **GAMALIEL BAILEY INTRODUCES HIS *NATIONAL ERA* TO A SOUTHERN WHITE AUDIENCE, 1847**

Unlike Smith and Garnet, Gamaliel Bailey never openly advocated an abolitionist–slave alliance. Diplomatic and usually mild, he opposed the use of violent and illegal tactics in the antislavery cause. As he explained in the inaugural issue of the National Era, *which he published in the slaveholding city of Washington, DC, he aimed to engage a southern audience and expand the Liberty party into that region.*

It has been said by foreigners that Americans are tolerant upon all subjects except that of slavery; that upon this question they are apt to be sensitive, excitable, prescriptive. There was a time when the remark was true with little qualification; and it may still be made with justice of certain classes of our population. But a better feeling is beginning to prevail. The spirit of 'toleration' displayed upon questions of politics and religion, generally, is gradually infusing itself into the discussion of the question of slavery. A majority of the anti-slavery people of the free States, without abating their zeal, or compromising their principles, clearly see that mere denunciation may inflame, but not convince – may terrify the cowardly, but must arouse the indignation and resistance of men of courage and intelligence. At this age of the world, people are too clear-sighted to mistake the invectives of human passion for the anathemas of inspiration. On the other hand, there are Southern men who feel in their hearts that the haughty claim that slavery shall be exempt from investigation, discussion, opposition, is a gross absurdity. They recognize in the anti-slavery men of the North honest advocates of human freedom, and are willing to listen to discussion, so that they be treated as men whose peculiar circumstances should not be lost sight of, and who have minds to be reasoned with, sensibilities to be respected.

Need we say that the leading object of the 'National Era' is to represent the class of anti-slavery men we have described, and to lay before the Southern men referred to such facts and arguments as may serve to throw further light upon the question of slavery, and its disposition? Particularly will it explain and enforce the doctrines and measures of the Liberty Party, urging them, not in the spirit of party, but in the love of the truth; not for the sake of obtaining numerical accessions to that party, but for the purpose of securing adherents to what it believes to be vital principle.

...

The Liberty Party, though at present confined to the free States, is not sectional in its creed or spirit: Its doctrines are American, its objects of universal interest, and it expects to find many more slave States following the example set them by their brethren in Western Virginia [where a small Liberty party had been established]. Nor does it confound the prerogatives of the State and Federal Governments. It clearly understands the rights and duties of the former, and the restrictions imposed on the latter. It does not propose to repeal the Black Laws of Ohio by action of Congress ... but by the action of its members resident in that State. So far as slavery may exist by act of Congress, affect Federal legislation or general politics, it will act against it by federative powers; but where it exists by the law and within the jurisdiction of the State, it leaves its members in that State to resort to State legislative or judicial action for its removal, seconding their efforts by the moral influence of the rest of the organization.

Gamaliel Bailey, [12], January 7, 1847.

DOCUMENT 14   FREDERICK DOUGLASS COMMENTS ON THE
FIRST WOMEN'S RIGHTS CONVENTION, 1848

Although feminism grew out of abolitionism, some male abolitionists were more favorable to women's rights than others were. Among the more outspoken was Frederick Douglass, the black orator and journalist. He attended the women's rights convention held at Seneca Falls, New York and published the following comments in his North Star.

One of the most interesting events of the past week, was the holding of what is technically styled a Women's Rights Convention at Seneca Falls.

The speaking, addresses, and resolutions of this extraordinary meeting was [*sic*] almost wholly conducted by women; and although they evidently felt themselves in a novel position, it is but simple justice to say that their whole proceedings were characterized by marked ability and dignity. No one present, we think, however much he might be disposed to differ from the views advanced by the leading speakers on that occasion, will fail to give them credit for brilliant talents and excellent dispositions. In this meeting, as in other deliberative assemblies, there were frequent differences of opinion and animated discussion; but in no case was there the slightest absence of good feeling and decorum. Several interesting documents setting forth the rights as well as the grievances of women were read. Among these was a Declaration of Sentiments, to be regarded as the basis of a grand movement for attaining the civil, social, political, and religious rights of women. We should not do justice to our own convictions, or to the excellent persons connected with this infant movement, if we did not in this connection offer a few remarks on the general subject which the convention met to consider and the objects they seek to attain. In doing so, we are not insensible that the bare mention of this truly important subject in any other than terms of contemptuous ridicule and scornful disfavor, is likely to excite against us the fury of *bigotry* and the folly of prejudice. A discussion of the rights of animals would be regarded with far more complacency by many of what are called the *wise* and the *good* of our land, than would a discussion of the rights of women. It is, in their estimation, to be guilty of evil thoughts, to think that woman is entitled to equal rights with man. Many who have at last made the discovery that the Negroes have some rights as well as other members of the human family, have yet to be convinced that women are entitled to any. Eight years ago a number of persons of this description actually abandoned the anti-slavery cause, lest by giving their influence in that direction they might possibly be giving countenance to the dangerous heresy that woman, in respect to rights, stands on an equal footing with man. In the judgement of such persons the American slave system, with all its concomitant horrors, is less to be deplored than this *wicked* idea. It is perhaps needless to say, that we cherish little sympathy for such sentiments or respect for such prejudices. Standing as we do upon the watch-tower of human freedom, we cannot be deterred from an expression of our approbation of any movement, however humble, to improve and elevate the character of any members of the human family. While it is impossible for us to go into this subject at length, and dispose of the various objections which are often urged against such a doctrine as that of female equality, we are free to say that in respect to political rights, we hold woman to be justly entitled to all we claim for man. We go farther, and express our conviction that all political rights which it is expedient for man to exercise, it is equally so for women. All that distinguishes man as an intelligent and accountable being, is equally true of woman, and if that government only is just which governs by the free consent of the governed, there can be no reason in the world for denying to woman the exercise of the elective franchise, or a hand in making and administering the laws of the land. Our doctrine is that 'right is of no sex.' We therefore bid the women engaged in this movement our humble Godspeed.

Frederick Douglass, [14], July 28, 1848.

DOCUMENT 15   SOJOURNER TRUTH ON WOMEN'S RIGHTS, 1851

A former New York slave and evangelical preacher, Sojourner Truth emerged during the late 1840s and 1850s as a popular speaker on behalf of black and women's rights. She used appearances before white audiences to establish herself as a symbol of strong black womanhood. The words she spoke at the women's rights convention held in Akron, Ohio in 1851 were later embellished, but the following contemporary transcription by Marius Robinson is probably more accurate.

May I say a few words? ... I want to say few words about the matter. I am a woman's rights. I have as much muscle as any man, and can do as much work as any man. I have plowed and reaped and husked and chopped and mowed, and can any man do more than that? I have heard much about the sexes being equal; I can carry as much as any man, and can eat as much too, if I can get it. I am as strong as any man that is now. As for intellect, all I can say is, if a woman have a pint and man a quart – why cant she have her little pint full? You need not be afraid to give us our rights for fear we will take too much – for we cant take more than our pint'll hold. The poor men seem to be all in confusion, and dont know what to do. Why children, if you have woman's rights give it to her and you will feel better. You will have your own rights, and they wont be so much trouble. I cant read, but I can hear. I have heard the bible and have learned that Eve caused man to sin. Well if woman upset the world, do give her a chance to set it right side up again. The lady has spoken about Jesus, how he never spurned woman from him, and she was right. When Lazarus died, Mary and Martha came to him with faith and love and besought him to raise their brother. And Jesus wept – and Lazarus came forth. And how came Jesus into the world? Through God who created him and woman who bore him. Man, where is your part? But the woman are coming up blessed be God and a few of the men are coming up with them. But [the white] man is in a tight place; the poor slave is on him, woman is coming on him, and he is surely between a hawk and a buzzard.

Sojourner Truth, [6], June 21, 1851.

DOCUMENT 16   FRANKLIN B. SANBORN PRESENTS JOHN
BROWN'S VIOLENT COMMITMENT TO EQUAL
RIGHTS, 1857–59

Franklin B. Sanborn was a member of the transcendentalist community in Concord, Massachusetts and an abolitionist supporter of John Brown's plan to lead a slave rebellion. Looking back over a quarter-century, Sanborn quotes Brown's last words before his execution and Brown's 1857 comments on the religious roots of his commitment to violent means.

Possibly the very last paper written by John Brown was this sentence, which he handed to one of his guards in the jail on the morning of his execution: –

CHARLESTOWN, VA., Dec. 2, 1859.

I, John Brown, am now quite *certain* that the crimes of this *guilty land* will never be purged away but with *blood*. I had, as I now think vainly, flattered myself that without very much bloodshed it might be done.

'Without the shedding of blood there is no remission of sins.' This was John Brown's old-fashioned theology, which the nation was so soon to verify by a fierce but salutary civil war. In my earliest serious conversation with him, in January, 1857, when he assured me that Christ's Golden rule and Jefferson's Declaration meant the same thing, he said further: 'I have always been delighted with the doctrine that all men are created equal; and to my mind it is like the Saviour's command, "Thou shalt love thy neighbor as thyself," for how can we do that unless our neighbor is equal to ourself? That is the doctrine, sir; and rather than have that fail in the world, or in these States, 't would be better for a whole generation to die a violent death. Better that heaven and earth pass away than that one jot or one tittle of this be not fulfilled.' Such was the faith in which he died.

Franklin B. Sanborn, ed., [34], p. 620.

DOCUMENT 17   WENDELL PHILLIPS REFLECTS ON THE ELECTION
OF ABRAHAM LINCOLN, 1860

Perhaps the most riveting orator of his time, Garrisonian leader Wendell Phillips of Boston became the North's most popular speaker during the Civil War. In this address delivered at Boston's Tremont Temple days after the election of 1860, Phillips analyzes the relationship of President-elect Abraham Lincoln to the abolitionists and especially to John Brown.

LADIES AND GENTLEMEN: If the telegraph speaks truth, for the first time in our history the *slave* has chosen a President of the United States.

{Cheers.} We have passed the Rubicon, for Mr. Lincoln rules to-day as much as he will after the 4th of March. It is the moral effect of this victory, not anything which his administration can or will probably do, that gives value to this success. Not an Abolitionist, hardly an antislavery man, Mr. Lincoln consents to represent an antislavery idea. A pawn on the political chessboard, his value is in his position; with fair effort, we may soon change him for knight, bishop, or queen, and sweep the board. {Applause.} This position he owes to no merit of his own, but to lives that have roused the nation's conscience, and deeds that have ploughed deep into its heart. ... There was great noise at [the Republican convention in] Chicago, much pulling of wires and creaking of wheels, then forth steps Abraham Lincoln. But John Brown was behind the curtain, and the cannon of March 4th will only echo the rifles at Harper's Ferry. Last year, we stood looking sadly at that gibbet against the Virginia sky. One turn of the kaleidoscope, – it is Lincoln in the balcony of the Capitol, and a million of hearts beating welcome below. {Cheers.}

Mr. [William H.] Seward [of New York] said, in 1850: 'You may slay the Wilmot Proviso in the Senate-Chamber, and bury it beneath the Capitol, to-day; the dead corpse, in complete steel, will haunt your legislative halls to-morrow.' They slew the martyr-chief on the banks of the Potomac; we buried his dust beneath the snows of North Elba; and the statesman Senator of New York wrote for his epitaph, 'Justly hung,' while party chiefs cried, 'Amen!' but one of those dead hands smote to ruin the Babylon which that Senator's ambition had builded, and the other lifts into the Capitol the President of 1861. {Applause.}

...

Notwithstanding the emptiness of Mr. Lincoln's mind, I think we shall yet succeed in making this a decent land to live in. {Cheers.} May I tell you why? Place yourselves at the door of the Chicago Convention. Do you see Mr. Lincoln? he believes a negro may walk where he wishes, eat what he earns, read what he can, and associate with any other who is exactly of the same shade of black as he is. That is all he can grant. Well, on the other side is Mr. Seward. He believes the free negro should sit on juries, vote, be eligible to office, – that's all. So much he thinks he can grant without hurting the Union.

Now raise your eyes up! In the blue sky above, you will see Mr. Garrison and John Brown! {Prolonged cheering.} They believe the negro, bond or free, has the same right to fight that a white man has, – the same claim on us to fight for him; and as for the consequences to the Union, who cares? Liberty first, and the Union afterward, is their motto. {Cheers.} Liberty first, and, as the Scotch say, 'Let them care who come ahind.'

Wendell Phillips, [31], pp. 294–318.

DOCUMENT 18   FREDERICK DOUGLASS URGES BLACK MEN TO ENLIST IN A UNION WAR FOR EMANCIPATION, 1863

Frederick Douglass had endorsed Garrisonian nonviolence and continued to have reservations concerning the effectiveness of antislavery violence throughout the 1850s. But he based his argument for black service in Union armies on a legacy of abolitionist admiration of slave rebels and John Brown.

When first the rebel cannon shattered the walls of Sumter, and drove away its starving garrison, I predicted that the war then and there inaugurated would not be fought out entirely by white men. Every month's experience during these two dreary years, has confirmed that opinion. A war undertaken and brazenly carried on for the perpetual enslavement of colored men, calls logically and loudly upon colored men to help suppress it. Only a moderate share of sagacity was needed to see that the arm of the slave was the best defence against the arm of the slaveholder. Hence with every reverse to the National arms, with every exulting shout of victory raised by the slaveholding rebels, I have implored the imperiled nation to unchain against her foes her powerful black hand. Slowly and reluctantly that appeal is beginning to be heeded. Stop not now to complain that it was not heeded sooner. ... Action! Action! not criticism, is the plain duty of this hour. ... Liberty won by white men would lose half its luster. Who would be free themselves must strike the blow. Better even die free, than to live slaves. This is the sentiment of every brave colored man amongst us. ...

...

The day dawns – the morning star is bright upon the horizon! The iron gate of our prison stands half open. One gallant rush from the North will fling it wide open, while four millions of our brothers and sisters shall march out into liberty. The chance is now given you to end in a day the bondage of centuries, and to rise in one bound from social degradation to the plane of common equality with all other varieties of men. Remember Denmark Vesey of Charleston. – Remember Nathaniel Turner of South Hampton [*sic*], remember Shields Green and [John] Copeland who followed noble John Brown, and fell as glorious martyrs for the cause of the slave. – Remember that in a contest with oppression, the Almighty has no attribute which can take sides with oppressors. The case is before you. This is our golden opportunity – let us accept it – and forever wipe out the dark reproaches unsparingly hurled against us by our enemies. [Let us] win for ourselves the gratitude of the country – and the best blessings of our posterity through all time. ...

'Men of Color, To Arms', [8], p. 802.

CHRONOLOGY

1619	First Africans arrive in British North America.
1676	Bacon's Rebellion.
1712	New York City slave revolt.
1739	Stono Rebellion in South Carolina.
1758	Quakers meeting in Philadelphia condemn slaveholders.
1775	First antislavery society is organized.
1776	United States Declaration of Independence.
1783	Abolition begins in the North.
1787	Slavery is banned in the Northwest Territory.
1791	Haitian Revolution begins.
1793	First fugitive slave law.
1800	Gabriel's conspiracy in Virginia.
1811	Slave revolt in Louisiana.
1816	American Colonization Society is organized.
1820	Missouri Compromise.
1822	Denmark Vesey's conspiracy in Charleston, South Carolina.
1829	David Walker publishes his *Appeal*.
1831	Nat Turner's revolt, Virginia.
1833	American Anti-Slavery Society is founded.
1835	Abolitionist postal campaign.
1836	House of Representatives passes the Gag Rule.
1839	*Amistad* slave revolt.
1840	American and Foreign Anti-Slavery Society is established. Liberty party is organized.
1841	*Creole* slave revolt.
1844	House of Representatives repeals the Gag Rule.
1846	War against Mexico begins. American Missionary Association is formed.
1848	Free Soil party is organized. Women's Rights Convention, Seneca Falls, New York.
1850	Compromise of 1850 is passed.
1851	Resistance to the Fugitive Slave Law of 1850 begins.
1854	Kansas–Nebraska Act is passed.

1856	Republican party is formed.
1857	Dred Scott case.
1859	John Brown's raid.
1861	The Civil War begins.
1863	Emancipation Proclamation is issued.
1865	Thirteenth Amendment is ratified.
1867	Fourteenth Amendment is ratified.
1870	Fifteenth Amendment is ratified. American Anti-Slavery Society dissolves.

GLOSSARY

Abolitionists Those who sought to end slavery within their colony, state, nation, or religious denomination.

Albany Patriot *(1843–48)* The official newspaper of the New York Anti-Slavery Society.

American Abolition Society (1855–60) The primary organization of the radical political abolitionists during the late 1850s. It absorbed the AFASS.

American Anti-Slavery Society (AASS, 1833–70) The national organization of immediate abolitionists during the 1830s. Garrisonians controlled it from 1840 until the Civil War.

American Colonization Society (ACS, 1816–1963) An organization that encouraged masters to free their slaves by proposing to send free blacks to Liberia in West Africa.

American Convention for Promoting the Abolition of Slavery and Improving the Condition of the African Race (1794-1838) A loose coalition of state and local societies dedicated to gradual abolition.

American and Foreign Anti-Slavery Society (AFASS, 1840–55) An organization of church-oriented abolitionists, who broke with the AASS in 1840.

American Missionary Association (AMA, 1846–present) An organization of church-oriented abolitionists that   supported antislavery missionaries in the slave states.

Antislavery A broad category of slavery's opponents, including abolitionists as well as those dedicated only to halting the territorial expansion of slavery.

Atlantic slave trade An international commerce in slaves between Africa and the Americas which lasted from the early 1500s into the 1800s.

Benevolence Charitable work undertaken by Christians, especially in response to the Second Great Awakening.

Biracialism Refers to cooperation across racial lines. Among abolitionists, it involved cooperation between blacks and whites against slavery and on behalf of racial justice.

Border South The area including the slave states of Delaware, Maryland, Virginia, Kentucky, and Missouri – as well as the District of Columbia – that bordered on the free states of Pennsylvania, Ohio, Indiana, and Illinois.

The Chesapeake The regions of Maryland and Virginia surrounding the Chesapeake Bay.

Colonizationists Those who contended that abolition could be accomplished only in conjunction with sending emancipated slaves to Africa or some other location beyond the borders of the United States.

Colored American *(New York, 1837–42)* The leading African-American newspaper of its period.

Dred Scott *v.* Sanford *(1857)* A Supreme Court case in which the court ruled that blacks were not United States citizens and that slavery was legal in all United States territories.

Emancipator *(New York, 1833–41; Boston, 1841–48)* A weekly newspaper that until 1840 served as the official organ of the AASS. Thereafter, it represented the Massachusetts Abolition Society and the Liberty party.

Enlightenment An intellectual movement centered in late-seventeenth and eighteenth-century Europe that sought to discover natural laws.

Evangelicals Protestants who emphasized faith rather than ritual and who sought to redeem the world through conversions.

Feminists Individuals, both female and male, who advocated equal rights for women.

Freedmen's Bureau (1865–68) A United States government agency that had power to aid, educate, and protect newly emancipated African Americans.

Free Soil party (1848–53) A political coalition against the expansion of slavery. It was composed of some northern Whigs, some northern Democrats, and most Liberty abolitionists.

Fugitive slave laws There were two of these. The law passed by Congress in 1793 allowed masters to recapture escaped slaves in the free states. The stronger law of 1850 relied on federal officials for enforcement and made aiding slaves to escape a federal offense.

Garrisonians Associates of William Lloyd Garrison, who by the early 1840s advocated disunion as the key to abolition.

Great Awakening A religious revival centered in Britain's North American colonies during the mid-eighteenth century.

Immediatists Those abolitionists who advocated, on moral principles, the immediate emancipation of the slaves and equal rights for African Americans within the United States.

Industrial Revolution A technological transformation based on the steam engine that altered modes of production and caused profound social change in Europe and the United States.

Liberator *(Boston, 1831–65)* William Lloyd Garrison's weekly newspaper.

Liberty party (1840–48) The first antislavery political party. Most of its supporters joined the Free Soil party in 1848, although radical political abolitionists continued to use the Liberty name into the 1850s.

Manumission An individual act of emancipation in which a master frees a slave through deed or will.

Massachusetts Abolition Society (1839–c. 1843) An organization established by church-oriented abolitionists in opposition to the Garrisonian Massachusetts Anti-Slavery Society.

Massachusetts Anti-Slavery Society (MASS, 1835–70) Succeeded the New England Anti-Slavery Society as the AASS auxiliary in Massachusetts.

Mission Institute Established in Quincy, Illinois by David Nelson during the late 1830s, it became a center of underground railroad activities.

National Anti-Slavery Standard *(New York, 1841–70)* The official weekly newspaper of the Garrisonian-dominated AASS.

National Era *(Washington, 1847–60)* Gamaliel Bailey's weekly newspaper. It supported in turn the Liberty, Free Soil, and Republican parties.

New England Anti-Slavery Society (NEASS, 1832–34) This was the first immediatist group organized by William Lloyd Garrison.

Nonextensionists Those who opposed only the territorial expansion of slavery.

Old Northwest Refers to the region of the United States formed out of the Northwest Territory. It includes the states of Ohio, Indiana, Illinois, Michigan, and Wisconsin.

Philadelphia Female Anti-Slavery Society (PFASS, 1833–70) A biracial organization established by Lucretia Mott and other Quaker women as an adjunct of the AASS.

Popular Sovereignty The policy adopted by the Democratic party in 1848 that would allow the actual settlers of each United States territory to legalize or prohibit slavery.

Quakers Members of the Society of Friends, a religious denomination that was established in England in 1647 and spread to America.

Radical Political Abolitionists Those who maintained that the United States Constitution made slavery illegal throughout the country.

Radical Republicans Antislavery politicians closely associated with abolitionists.

Second Great Awakening A religious revival centered in the North and upper South during the early decades of the nineteenth century.

'*The Seventy*' A group of young antislavery agents trained by Theodore D. Weld in 1836.

Slave power A term used to indicate the political control exercised by slaveholders over the United States government.

Southern Press *(Washington, 1850–51)* A daily newspaper established by southern members of Congress to serve the proslavery cause in opposition to the *National Era*.

Underground railroad Refers to several loosely organized semi-secret biracial networks that helped slaves escape from the border South to the North and Canada.

Wesleyan Methodist Connection An abolitionist church formed in 1842 by seceders from the Methodist Episcopal Church.

WHO'S WHO

Adams, John Quincy (1767–1848) A former United States president who, as a member of Congress from Massachusetts, led the struggle to repeal the Gag Rule.

Allen, Richard (1760–1831) The principal founder of the AME Church and of Philadelphia's Free African Society. His career as an abolitionist stretched from 1793 to 1830.

Bailey, Gamaliel (1807–59) He organized the Ohio Liberty party in 1840 and later supported the Free Soil and Republican parties. He edited the *Philanthropist* (Cincinnati, 1837–46) and the *National Era* (Washington, 1847–59).

Barbadoes, James G. (c. 1796–1841) He emerged in Boston as a black abolitionist during the 1820s. He helped establish the AASS and integrated the NEASS in 1833.

Benezet, Anthony (1713–84) A Quaker abolitionist who wrote against slavery and the Atlantic slave trade and helped persuade Pennsylvanians to adopt gradual abolition in 1780.

Bibb, Henry (1815–54) An escaped slave who became an abolitionist speaker in 1844. He was active in Michigan, Ohio, and Canada and supported the AFASS and the AMA.

Bigelow, Jacob (1790–?) A white attorney who, during the 1850s, was the leader of underground railroad efforts in Washington, DC.

Birney, James G. (1792–1857) A former Alabama slaveholder who became the Liberty candidate for president in 1840 and 1844.

Brown, John (1800–59) A practical abolitionist closely allied with the radical political abolitionists. He is best known for his raid on Harpers Ferry, Virginia in 1859.

Brown, William Wells (1814?–84) An escaped slave who became an active abolitionist in Cleveland, Ohio during the early 1840s. Brown was the first African American to publish a novel.

Cary, Mary Ann Shadd (1823–93) The editor of the *Provincial Freeman* in Toronto and a leading advocate of black settlement in Canada West (Ontario). Born free in Wilmington, Delaware, she spoke widely in the North.

Chandler, Elizabeth Margaret (1807–34) A Quaker poet who wrote for Benjamin Lundy's *Genius of Universal Emancipation*. She had appealed to women to become abolitionists.

Chaplin, William L. (c. 1795–1871) The general agent of the New York Anti-Slavery Society during the late 1830s and 1840s. During the late 1840s, he was editor of the *Albany Patriot* and helped slaves escape from Washington, DC.

Chapman, Maria Weston (1806–85) From Boston, she was a white Garrisonian. She managed antislavery fairs and served on the executive committee of the AASS.

Chase, Salmon P. (1808–73) From Ohio, he was the most prominent of the political abolitionists. He led most Liberty abolitionists into the Free Soil party in 1848 and helped lead the Republican party during the 1850s and 1860s.

Child, Lydia Maria (1802–80) From Massachusetts, she was a prominent white Garrisonian advocate of moral suasion. She edited the *National Anti-Slavery Standard* from 1841 to 1844.

Clay, Cassius Marcellus (1810–1903) From Kentucky, he was the most prominent southern white abolitionist. He maintained ties to northern abolitionists and supported the Free Soil and Republican parties.

Cornish, Samuel E. (c. 1795–1858) Co-editor, with John Russwurm, of *Freedom's Journal* (1827–29) and sole editor of the *Colored American* (1837–39).

Cuffe, Paul (1759–1817) A wealthy sea captain who was the most prominent black advocate of African colonization during the first two decades of the nineteenth century.

Delany, Martin R. (1812–85) The leading black advocate of African colonization during the 1850s. He served during the Civil War as one of the few black commissioned officers.

Deslondes, Charles (?–1811) Probably born in Haiti, he led the Louisiana slave revolt of 1811.

Douglass, Frederick (1818–95) The most prominent black abolitionist. He edited the *North Star* (Rochester, 1847–51) and *Frederick Douglass' Paper* (Rochester, 1851–60).

Douglass, Sarah Mapps (1806–82) A black teacher who became an abolitionist and feminist. She helped establish Philadelphia's Female Anti-Slavery Society in 1833.

Fee, John G. (1816–1901) A white church-oriented Kentucky abolitionist who, during the course of his career, allied himself with the AFASS, AMA, and – by the mid-1850s – the radical political abolitionists.

Foster, Abigail Kelley (1811–87) A white Garrisonian and advocate of women's rights. Her appointment to the AASS program committee in 1840 was the immediate cause of the disruption of that organization.

Forten, James (1766–1842) A prosperous black entrepreneur in Philadelphia who became an abolitionist in 1799. He criticized the ACS during the 1820s and was an early supporter of William Lloyd Garrison.

Forten, Sarah (1814–83) Daughter of James Forten. With her mother and sisters, she helped establish Philadelphia's Female Anti-Slavery Society in 1833.

Freeman, Elizabeth (c. 1742–1829) A Massachusetts slave who sued for her freedom in 1781. Her case had a substantial impact on the Massachusetts supreme court ruling abolishing slavery in that state.

Gabriel (1776–1800) A slave blacksmith who planned a massive but aborted slave revolt near Richmond, Virginia in 1800.

Garnet, Henry Highland (1815–82) A former slave who became a radical political abolitionist and is best known for his militant 'Address to the Slaves' in 1843.

Garrison, William Lloyd (1805–79) He was chiefly responsible for initiating immediate abolitionism in the United States. By the late 1830s, he advocated nonresistance and women's rights as well as abolition in his weekly *Liberator*.

Giddings, Joshua R. (1795–1864) He represented Ohio's staunchly antislavery Western Reserve in Congress from 1839 to 1859.

Green, Beriah (1795–1874) He was among the white founders of the AASS and later became a radical political abolitionist. During the 1830s he was president of Oneida Institute, in central New York.

Grimké, Sarah (1792–1873) A native of South Carolina who, with her sister Angelina, helped associate abolitionism with women's rights during the 1830s.

Hall, Prince (1735–1807) The most prominent African-American abolitionist of the late eighteenth century. A slave until 1770, he campaigned on behalf of abolition in Massachusetts, promoted black schools, and opposed the slave trade.

Harper, Frances Ellen Watkins (1825–1911) Born free in Baltimore, during the 1850s she published antislavery poetry and traveled across the North as an antislavery speaker.

Henson, Josiah (1789–1883) He escaped from slavery in Maryland in 1830. He settled in Canada West and during the 1840s made several forays into the South to help other slaves escape.

Higginson, Thomas Wentworth (1823–1911) A white Unitarian minister who violently resisted the Fugitive Slave Law of 1850 and cooperated with John Brown. During the Civil War, he commanded a black Union regiment.

Holly, Myron (1779–1841) From western New York, he was the leading advocate during the late 1830s of forming an abolitionist political party. His efforts led to the creation in 1840 of what became the Liberty party.

Janney, Samuel M. (1801–80) A moderate Quaker abolitionist who was active in northern Virginia from the 1820s through to the Civil War.

Jones, Absalom (1746–1818) A former slave, a founder of Philadelphia's Free African Society, and a leader in the movement to establish separate black churches.

Lay, Benjamin (1681?–1759) A pioneer Quaker abolitionist in Barbados and Pennsylvania. He disrupted Quaker meetings to draw attention to the sinfulness and oppressiveness of slaveholding.

Leavitt, Joshua (1794–1873) A white church-oriented abolitionist who edited the *New York Evangelist* (1831–37) and the *Emancipator* (New York and Boston, 1837–48). He helped lead the Liberty party during the 1840s.

Loguen, Jermain Wesley (c. 1813–72) An escaped slave who became an abolitionist in western New York during the early 1840s. He was a radical political abolitionist and was active in the underground railroad.

Lovejoy, Elijah P. (1802–37) A white abolitionist who published his *Observer* in St Louis and later in Alton, Illinois. He became a martyr to the cause after an antiabolition mob killed him.

Lundy, Benjamin (1789–1839) A northern-born Quaker who published his *Genius of Universal Emancipation* (1821–33) in such southern cities as Baltimore and Washington.

Miner, Myrtilla (1815–64) A white teacher from New York who had ties to the radical political abolitionists. During the 1850s she conducted a school for black girls in Washington, DC.

Mott, Lucretia (1793–1880) From Philadelphia, she was a Quaker abolitionist and a loyal Garrisonian. She is best known for her role in calling the Seneca Falls Women's Rights Convention in 1848.

Nelson, David (1793–1844) A former slaveholder from Tennessee who attempted to introduce immediate abolitionism into Missouri in 1836. He later founded the Mission Institute in Quincy, Illinois.

Parker, John P. (1827–1900) He purchased his freedom in Alabama in 1845 and settled in Ripley, Ohio in 1849. For the next fifteen years he helped slaves escape from Kentucky.

Parker, Theodore (1810–60) From Massachusetts, he was a prominent white Unitarian minister and second-generation abolitionist who resisted enforcement of the Fugitive Slave Law of 1850 and supported John Brown's efforts.

Phillips, Wendell (1811–86) An aristocratic white Bostonian and the most brilliant of the abolitionist orators. Until 1865 he was a close ally of William Lloyd Garrison.

Purvis, Robert (1810–98) From Philadelphia, he was a black Garrisonian who had been born free in South Carolina. He served as vice president of the AASS from 1841 to 1865 and provided extensive aid to fugitive slaves.

Rankin, John (1793–1886) A white native of Tennessee, he became an abolitionist during the 1820s. He is best known for his underground railroad work in and about Ripley, Ohio.

Remond, Charles Lenox (1810–73) The first African American to be employed as an AASS lecturer. Born in Massachusetts, he remained a Garrisonian throughout the antebellum period.

Remond, Sarah Parker (1826–94) The sister of Charles Lenox Remond. She toured in the North and Great Britain as an antislavery speaker during the 1840s and 1850s.

Rush, Benjamin (1746–1813) A white physician and scientist who served as president of the Pennsylvania Society for Promoting the Abolition of Slavery during the late 1700s.

Smallwood, Thomas (1801–?) Born into slavery in Maryland, he purchased his freedom in 1831. In 1841 he joined Charles T. Torrey in establishing an underground railroad network leading north from Washington, DC.

Smith, Gerrit (1797–1874) The leader of the radical political abolitionists. A very wealthy white resident of western New York, he influenced nearly every aspect of abolitionism.

Snodgrass, Joseph Evans (1813–80) From Baltimore, he was a white antislavery journalist who, during the 1840s, advocated both abolition and equal rights for free African Americans.

Stanton, Elizabeth Cady (1815–1902) A white Garrisonian feminist, married to Henry B. Stanton, who broke with Garrison in 1837. She helped organize the Seneca Falls Women's Rights Convention of 1848.

Stanton, Henry B. (1805–87) From Massachusetts and New York, he became an abolitionist in 1834. A leader of the AASS during the 1830s, he became a political abolitionist during the late 1830s.

Stewart, Alvan (1790–1849) From New York, he was an early advocate of an abolitionist political party. A white attorney, he pioneered the radical political abolitionist interpretation of the United States Constitution.

Stewart, Maria W. (1803–79) She gained notoriety in Boston during the early 1830s as a black advocate of abolition, racial equality, and women's rights.

Still, William (1821–1902) From Philadelphia, he was a son of former slaves and coordinated underground railroading between the Chesapeake and Canada during the 1850s.

Swisshelm, Jane Grey (1815–84) An independent and relatively conservative white advocate of abolition and women's rights. She published newspapers in Pittsburgh and Minnesota during the 1840s and 1850s.

Tappan, Arthur (1786–1865) A wealthy white New York City merchant who became an evangelical abolitionist and philanthropist. He served as the first president of the AASS.

Tappan, Lewis (1788–1873 Like his brother Arthur, he was a wealthy merchant whose evangelical beliefs led him to immediatism. Of the two, Lewis was by far the more able and influential.

Thayer, Eli (1819–99) A white Massachusetts entrepreneur, he promoted free state settlement in Kansas Territory and joined John C. Underwood in attempting to establish free-labor settlements in Virginia during the 1850s.

Torrey, Charles T. (1813–46) A white radical political abolitionist who became an antislavery martyr when he died while serving a prison term in Maryland for helping slaves escape.

Truth, Sojourner (c. 1799–1883) The most prominent of black women who became abolitionist and feminist orators. Born into slavery in New York, she gained her freedom in 1826.

Tubman, Harriet (c. 1820–1913) The best known of the underground railroad conductors. After escaping from slavery in Maryland in 1849, she returned many times to lead others northward.

Underwood, John C. (1809–73) He gained prominence during the 1850s as an advocate of free-labor colonization of Virginia. A former Liberty abolitionist, he supported in turn the Free Soil and Republican parties.

Vesey, Denmark (1767?–1822) A former Haitian slave who led a failed slave revolt conspiracy in Charleston, South Carolina.

Walker, David (1796?–1830) A free African American from North Carolina who, in Boston in 1829, published his *Appeal to the Colored Citizens of the World*, which helped shape immediate abolitionism in the United States.

Ward, Samuel Ringgold (1817–c. 1866) An escaped slave from Maryland who became an abolitionist in New York City in 1834. After 1840 he was active in the AFASS, AMA, Liberty party, and Free Soil party.

Washington, Madison (1810?–?) He led the November 1841 slave revolt aboard the *Creole* as it attempted to sail from Richmond, Virginia to New Orleans.

Webster, Delia A. (1817–1904) A white teacher from Vermont who was convicted in Kentucky in 1844 on charges of having helped slaves escape. During the 1850s she attempted to establish a free-labor colony in that state.

Weld, Angelina Grimké (1805–79) Born in South Carolina to a slaveholding family, with her sister Sarah, she gained notoriety during the 1830s as one of the first women to speak publicly on behalf of abolition.

Weld, Theodore Dwight (1803–95) A prominent white abolitionist of the 1830s. He led the antislavery debate at Lane Seminary and spread immediatism through the Old Northwest.

Whipper, William (1804–76) From Pennsylvania, he was a prominent black abolitionist and underground railroad activist. He was a Garrisonian through the 1840s, then became more sympathetic to black nationalism.

Woolman, John (1720–72) A pioneer Quaker abolitionist. In cooperation with Anthony Benezet, he persuaded the Philadelphia Yearly Meeting to oppose slaveholding.

Wright, Elizur Jr (1804–85) A white reformer from Massachusetts who was national secretary of the AASS during the 1830s. Thereafter he was an independent political abolitionist.

BIBLIOGRAPHY

PRIMARY SOURCES: MANUSCRIPT

1 Bettie Browne to Emily Howland, July 3, 1859, Howland Papers, Cornell University, Ithaca, New York.
2 Abigail Kelley Foster to Maria Weston Chapman, October 5, 1847, Chapman Papers, Boston Public Library.
3 Myrtilla Miner to Gerrit Smith, February 11, 1850, Miner Papers, Library of Congress.

PRIMARY SOURCES: NEWSPAPERS AND PERIODICALS

4 *Albany Patriot*, (a) June 15, 1843; (b) August 13, 1845; (c) May 20, 1846.
5 *American Missionary* (New York), (a) June 1857; (b) September 1858.
6 *Anti-Slavery Bugle* (Salem, Ohio), June 21, 1851.
7 *Colored American* (Philadelphia), March 4, 1837.
8 *Douglass Monthly* (Rochester, NY), March 1863.
9 *Frederick Douglass' Paper* (Rochester, NY), (a) October 16, 1851; (b) February 12, 1852; (c) February 26, 1852.
10 *Liberator* (Boston), (a) September 17, 1831; (b) March 10, 1832; (c) July 25, 1835; (d) November 19, 1836; (e) June 8, 1838; (f) June 2, 1843; (g) November 6, 1857; (h) May 28, 1858.
11 *National Anti-Slavery Standard* (New York), August 10, 1843.
12 *National Era* (Washington, DC), (a) January 7, 1847; (b) February 21, 1850.
13 *National Republican* (Washington, DC), April 4, 1862.
14 *North Star* (Rochester, NY), July 28, 1848.
15 *Principia* (New York), December 21, 1861.

PRIMARY SOURCES: OTHER PRINTED MATERIALS

16 *Annals of Congress*, 4 Cong., 2 sess. (January 23, 1797), 2015–18.
17 Aptheker, Herbert, ed., '*One Continual Cry': David Walker's Appeal to the Colored Citizens of the World*. New York: Humanities, 1965.
18 Barnes, Gilbert H. and Dwight L. Dumond, eds, *The Letters of Theodore Weld, Angelina Grimké Weld, and Sarah Grimké, 1822–1844* (2 vols). 1934; reprint, Gloucester, MA: Peter Smith, 1965.
19 Child, Lydia Maria, *An Appeal in Favor of that Class of Americans Called Africans* (ed. Caroline L. Karcher). Amherst, MA: University of Massachusetts Press, 1996.
20 Clay, Cassius M., *The Writings of Cassius Marcellus Clay* (ed. Horace Greeley). 1848; reprint, New York: Negro Universities Press, 1969.

21   *Congressional Globe*, (a) 30 Cong., 1 sess., 501, 505; (b) 31 Cong., 1 sess., Appen. 1582–1630.

22   Finkenbine, Roy E., ed., *Sources of the African-American Past: Primary Sources in American History*. New York: Longman, 1997.

23   Garrison, William Lloyd, *Thoughts on African Colonization*. 1832; reprint, New York: Arno, 1968.

24   Grimké, Angelina E., 'Appeal to the Christian Women of the South', *Anti-Slavery Examiner* 1 (September 1836): 1–36.

25   Henson, Josiah, *'Truth Is Stranger than Fiction.' An Autobiography of the Rev Josiah Henson*. Boston: B.B. Russell, 1879.

26   Jefferson, Thomas, *Notes on the State of Virginia* (ed. William Peden). Chapel Hill, NC: University of North Carolina Press, 1954.

27   Merrill, Walter M. and Louis Ruchames, eds, *The Letters of William Lloyd Garrison* (6 vols). Cambridge, MA: Harvard University Press, 1971–81.

28   Meyer, Michael, ed., *Frederick Douglass: The Narrative and Selected Writings*. New York: Modern Library, 1984.

29   Parker, John P., *His Promised Land: The Autobiography of John P. Parker, Former Slave and Conductor on the Underground Railroad* (ed. Stuart Seely Sprague). New York: Norton, 1996.

30   Phelps, Amos A., *Lectures on Slavery and Its Remedy*. Boston: New England Anti-Slavery Society, 1834.

31   Phillips, Wendell, *Speeches, Lectures, and Letters*. 1884; reprint, New York: Negro Universities Press, 1969.

32   Ripley, E. Peter, et al., eds, *The Black Abolitionist Papers* (5 vols). Chapel Hill, NC: University of North Carolina Press, 1985–92.

33   Ruchames, Louis, ed., *The Abolitionists: A Collection of Their Writings*. New York: Capricorn Books, 1964.

34   Sanborn, Franklin B., ed., *The Life and Letters of John Brown, Liberator of Kansas, and Martyr of Virginia*.1885; reprint, New York: Negro Universities Press, 1969.

35   Thompson, George, *Prison Life and Reflections*. 1847; reprint, New York: Negro Universities Press, 1969.

36   Woolman, John, *Considerations on the Keeping of Negroes … 1762*, in *Works of John Woolman*. Philadelphia, PA: Joseph Crukshank, 1774.

SECONDARY SOURCES: BOOKS

37   Abzug, Robert H., *Passionate Liberator: Theodore Dwight Weld and the Dilemma of Reform*. New York: Oxford University Press, 1980.

38   Abzug, Robert H., *Cosmos Crumbling: American Reform and the Religious Imagination*. New York: Oxford University Press, 1994.

39   Aptheker, Herbert, *Abolitionism: A Revolutionary Movement*. Boston, MA: Twayne, 1989.

40   Aptheker, Herbert, *Anti-Racism in US History: The First Two Hundred Years*. New York: Greenwood, 1992.

41   Ashworth, John, *Slavery, Capitalism, and Politics in the Antebellum Republic*. New York: Cambridge University Press, 1995.

42   Barnes, Gilbert H., *The Antislavery Impulse, 1830–1844.* 1933; reprint Gloucester, MA: Peter Smith, 1973.

43   Bell, Howard, *A Survey of the Negro Convention Movement, 1830–1861.* New York: Arno, 1969.

44   Berlin, Ira, *Slaves without Masters: The Free Negro in the Antebellum South.* New York: Random House, 1974.

45   Berlin, Ira, *Many Thousands Gone: The First Two Centuries of Slavery in North America.* Cambridge, MA: Belknap Press, 1998.

46   Blackett, R.J.M., *Building an Antislavery Wall: Black Americans in the Atlantic Abolitionist Movement, 1830–1860.* Baton Rouge, LA: Louisiana State University Press, 1983.

47   Blue, Frederick J., *The Free Soilers: Third Party Politics, 1848–54.* Urbana, IL: University of Illinois Press, 1973.

48   Blue, Frederick J., *Salmon P. Chase: A Life in Politics.* Kent, OH: Kent State University Press, 1987.

49   Blue, Frederick J., *Charles Sumner and the Conscience of the North.* Arlington Heights, IL: Harlan Davidson, 1994.

50   Bradford, Sarah, *Scenes in the Life of Harriet Tubman.* 1869; reprint, Salem, NH: Ayer, 1992.

51   Brandt, Nat, *The Town that Started the Civil War.* Syracuse, NY: Syracuse University Press, 1990.

52   Brown, Letitia Woods, *Free Negroes in the District of Columbia, 1790–1846.* New York: Oxford University Press, 1972.

53   Brown, Richard, *Modernization: The Transformation of American Life, 1600–1865.* New York: Hill and Wang, 1976.

54   Campbell, Stanley W., *The Slave Catchers: Enforcement of the Fugitive Slave Law, 1850–1860.* Chapel Hill, NC: University of North Carolina Press, 1968.

55   Commanger, Henry Steele, *The Blue and the Grey* (revised edn, 2 vols). New York: Mentor, 1973. Vol. 1.

56   Cornish, Dudley T., *The Sable Arm: Negro Troops in the Union Army.* 1956; reprint, New York: Norton, 1966.

57   Cott, Nancy, *The Bonds of Womanhood: 'Woman's Sphere' in New England, 1785–1835.* New Haven, CT: Yale University Press, 1977.

58   Cross, Whitney, *The Burned-over District: The Social and Intellectual History of Religious Enthusiasm in Western New York, 1800–1850.* Ithaca, NY: Cornell University Press, 1950.

59   Davis, David Brion, *The Problem of Slavery in the Age of Revolution, 1770–1823.* Ithaca, NY: Cornell University Press, 1975.

60   Davis, David Brion, *Slavery and Human Progress.* New York: Oxford University Press, 1984.

61   Davis, Hugh, *Joshua Leavitt: Evangelical Abolitionist.* Baton Rouge, LA: Louisiana State University Press, 1990.

62   DeBoar, Clara Merritt, *Be Jubilant My Feet: African-American Abolitionists in the American Missionary Association, 1839–1861.* New York: Garland, 1994.

63   Dillon, Merton L., *Elijah P. Lovejoy, Abolitionist Editor.* Urbana, IL: University of Illinois Press, 1961.

64   Dillon, Merton L., *Benjamin Lundy and the Struggle for Negro Freedom.* Urbana, IL: University of Illinois Press, 1966.

65   Dillon, Merton L., *The Abolitionists: The Growth of a Dissenting Minority.* New York: Norton, 1974.

66   Dillon, Merton L., *Slavery Attacked: Southern Slaves and Their Allies, 1619–1865.* Baton Rouge, LA: Louisiana State University Press, 1990.

67   Donald, David, *Lincoln Reconsidered: Essays on the Civil War Era.* New York: Vintage, 1961.

68   Drake, Thomas E., *Quakers and Slavery in America.* New Haven, CT: Yale University Press, 1950.

69   Dubois, Ellen C., *Feminism and Suffrage: The Emergence of an Independent Women's Movement in America, 1848–1869.* Ithaca, NY: Cornell University Press, 1978.

70   Egerton, Douglas R., *Gabriel's Rebellion: The Virginia Slave Conspiracies of 1800 & 1802.* Chapel Hill, NC: University of North Carolina Press, 1993.

71   Egerton, Douglas R., *He Shall Go Out Free: The Lives of Denmark Vesey.* Madison, WI: Madison House, 1999.

72   Elkins, Stanley M., *Slavery: A Problem in American Institutional and Intellectual Life* (3rd edn). Chicago, IL: University of Chicago Press, 1976.

73   Essig, James D., *The Bonds of Wickedness: American Evangelicals against Slavery, 1770–1808.* Philadelphia, PA: Temple University Press, 1982.

74   Farrison, William Edward, *William Wells Brown: Author and Reformer.* Chicago, IL: University of Chicago Press, 1969.

75   Fehrenbacher, Don E., *The Dred Scott Case: Its Significance in American Law and Politics.* New York: Oxford University Press, 1978.

76   Filler, Louis, *The Crusade Against Slavery, 1830–1860.* New York: Harper and Row, 1960.

77   Finkelman, Paul, *An Imperfect Union: Slavery, Federalism, and Comity.* Chapel Hill, NC: University of North Carolina Press, 1991.

78   Finkelman, Paul, *Slavery and the Founders: Race and Liberty in the Age of Jefferson.* Armonk, NY: M.E. Sharpe, 1996.

79   Fladeland, Betty, *Men and Brothers: Anglo-American Anti-Slavery Cooperation.* Urbana, IL: University of Illinois Press, 1972.

80   Flexner, James Thomas, *George Washington: The Forge of Experience (1732–1775).* Boston, MA: Little, Brown, 1965.

81   Foner, Eric, *Free Soil, Free Labor, Free Men: The Ideology of the Republican Party before the Civil War.* New York: Oxford University Press, 1970.

82   Foner, Eric, *Reconstruction: America's Unfinished Revolution, 1863–1877.* New York: Oxford University Press, 1988.

83   Foner, Philip, *History of Black Americans, from Africa to the Emergence of the Cotton Kingdom.* Westport, CT: Greenwood, 1975.

84   Franklin, John Hope and Loren Schweninger, *Runaway Slaves: Rebels on the Plantation.* New York: Oxford University Press, 1999.

85   Frederickson, George M., *The Black Image in the White Mind: The Debate on Afro-American Character and Destiny, 1877–1964.* New York: Harper and Row, 1971.

86   Fredrickson, George M, *The Arrogance of Race: Historical Perspectives on Slavery, Racism, and Social Inequality.* Middleton, CT: Wesleyan University Press, 1988.

87 Friedman, Lawrence J., *Gregarious Saints: Self and Community in American Abolitionism, 1830–1870*. New York: Cambridge University Press, 1982.

88 Gara, Larry, *The Liberty Line: The Legend of the Underground Railroad*. Lexington, KY: University of Kentucky Press, 1961.

89 Garrison, Wendell Phillips and Francis Jackson Garrison, *William Lloyd Garrison, 1805–1889: The Story of His Life Told by His Children* (4 vols). New York: Century, 1885–89.

90 Genovese, Eugene D., *Roll, Jordon, Roll: The World the Slaves Made*. 1974; reprint, New York: Vintage Books, 1976.

91 Genovese, Eugene D., *From Rebellion to Revolution: Afro-American Slave Revolts in the Making of the Modern World*. Baton Rouge, LA: Louisiana State University Press, 1979.

92 Gienapp, William, *The Origins of the Republican Party, 1852–1856*. New York: Oxford University Press, 1987.

93 Ginsburg, Lori D., *Women and the Work of Benevolence: Morality, Politics, and Class in the Nineteenth Century United States*. New Haven, CT: Yale University Press, 1990.

94 Glassman-Hersh, Blanch, *Slavery of Sex: Feminist-Abolitionists in Nineteenth-Century America*. Urbana, IL: University of Illinois Press, 1978.

95 Glatthaar, Joseph, *Forged in Battle: The Civil War Alliance between Black Soldiers and White Officers*. New York: Free Press, 1990.

96 Goodman, Paul, *Of One Blood: Abolitionism and the Origins of Racial Equality*. Berkeley, CA: University of California Press, 1998.

97 Griffith, Cyril, *African Dream: Martin Delany and the Emergence of Pan-African Thought*. University Park, PA: Pennsylvania State University Press, 1975.

98 Griffith, Elizabeth, *In Her Own Right: The Life of Elizabeth Cady Stanton*. New York: Oxford University Press, 1984.

99 Grimsted, David, *American Mobbing, 1828–1865: Toward Civil War*. New York: Oxford University Press, 1998.

100 Harlow, Ralph V., *Gerrit Smith, Philanthropist and Reformer*. New York: Holt, 1939.

101 Harrold, Stanley, *Gamaliel Bailey and Antislavery Union*. Kent, OH: Kent State University Press, 1986.

102 Harrold, Stanley, *The Abolitionists and the South, 1831–1861*. Lexington, KY: University Press of Kentucky, 1995.

103 Hinks, Peter P., *To Awaken My Afflicted Brethren: David Walker and the Problem of Antebellum Slave Resistance*. University Park, PA: Pennsylvania State University Press, 1990.

104 Horton, James Oliver and Lois E. Horton, *In Hope of Liberty: Culture, Community, and Protest among Northern Free Blacks, 1700–1860*. New York: Oxford University Press, 1997.

105 Howard, Victor B., *The Evangelical War against Slavery and Caste: The Life and Times of John G. Fee*. Selinsgrove, PA: Susquehanna University Press, 1996.

106 Hunt, Alfred N., *Haiti's Influence on Antebellum America: Slumbering Volcano in the Caribbean*. Baton Rouge, LA: Louisiana State University Press, 1988.

107 Jacobs, Donald, ed., *Courage and Conscience: Black and White Abolitionists in Boston*. Bloomington, IN: Indiana University Press, 1993.

108   Jeffrey, Julie Roy, *The Great Silent Army of Abolitionists: Ordinary Women in the Antislavery Movement*. Chapel Hill, NC: University of North Carolina Press, 1998.

109   Johannsen, Robert W., *Stephen A. Douglas*. New York: Oxford University Press, 1973.

110   Johnson, Paul, *Shopkeepers' Millennium: Society and Revivals in Rochester, New York, 1815–1837*. New York: Hill and Wang, 1978.

111   Jones, Howard, *Mutiny on the Amistad: The Saga of a Slave Revolt and Its Impact on American Abolition, Law, and Diplomacy*. New York: Oxford University Press, 1986.

112   Kaplan, Sidney and Emma Nogrady Kaplan, *The Black Presence in the Era of the American Revolution*. Amherst, MA: University of Massachusetts Press, 1989.

113   Karcher, Carolyn L., *The First Woman of the Republic: A Cultural Biography of Lydia Maria Child*. Durham, NC: Duke University Press, 1996.

114   Kolchin, Peter, *American Slavery, 1619–1877*. New York: Hill and Wang, 1993.

115   Kraditor, Aileen S., *Means and Ends in American Abolitionism: Garrison and His Critics on Strategy and Tactics*. New York: Random House, 1967.

116   Kraut, Alan M., ed., *Crusaders and Compromisers: Essays on the Relationship of the Antislavery Struggle to the Antebellum Party System*. Westport, CT: Greenwood, 1983.

117   Lerner, Gerda, *The Grimke Sisters of South Carolina: Rebels against Slavery*. Boston, MA: Houghton Mifflin, 1967.

118   Lesick, Lawrence Thomas, *The Lane Rebels: Evangelicals and Antislavery in Antebellum America*. Metuchen, NJ: Scarecrow, 1980.

119   Levine, Bruce, *Half Slave and Half Free: The Roots of Civil War*. New York: Hill and Wang, 1993.

120   Litwack, Leon F., *North of Slavery: The Negro in the Free States, 1790–1860*. Chicago, IL: University of Chicago Press, 1961.

121   Mabee, Carlton, *Black Freedom: The Nonviolent Abolitionists from 1830 Through the Civil War*. London: Macmillan, 1970.

122   Martin, Waldo E. Jr, *The Mind of Frederick Douglass*. Chapel Hill, NC: University of North Carolina Press, 1984.

123   Mayer, Henry, *All on Fire: William Lloyd Garrison and the Abolition of Slavery*. New York: St Martin's Press, 1999.

124   McFeely, William S., *Frederick Douglass*. New York: Simon and Schuster, 1991.

125   McKivigan, John R., *The War against Proslavery Religion: Abolitionism and the Northern Churches, 1830–1865*. Ithaca, NY: Cornell University Press, 1984.

126   McKivigan, John R. and Stanley Harrold, eds, *Antislavery Violence: Sectional, Cultural, and Racial Conflict in Antebellum America*. Knoxville, TN: University of Tennessee Press, 1999.

127   McManus, Edgar J., *Black Bondage in the North*. Syracuse, NY: Syracuse University Press, 1988.

128   McPherson, James M., *The Struggle for Equality: Abolitionists and the Negro in the Civil War and Reconstruction*. 1964; reprint, Princeton, NJ: Princeton University Press, 1992.

129 McPherson, James M., *Battle Cry of Freedom: The Civil War Era*. New York: Ballantine, 1988.

130 McPherson, James M., *Ordeal by Fire: The Civil War and Reconstruction* (2nd edn). New York: McGraw-Hill, 1992.

131 McPherson, James M., *The Abolitionist Legacy: From Reconstruction to the NAACP* (2nd edn). Princeton, NJ: Princeton University Press, 1995.

132 Melish, Joanne Pope, *Disowning Slavery: Gradual Emancipation and 'Race' in New England, 1780–1860*. Ithaca, NY: Cornell University Press, 1998.

133 Miller, Floyd J., *The Search for Black Nationality: Black Colonization and Emigration, 1778–1863*. Urbana, IL: University of Illinois Press, 1975.

134 Miller, William Lee, *Arguing about Slavery: John Quincy Adams and the Great Battle in the United States Congress*. New York: Vintage, 1995.

135 Mintz, Steven, *Moralists and Modernizers: America's Pre-Civil War Reformers*. Baltimore, MD: Johns Hopkins University Press, 1995.

136 Mullin, Gerald, *Flight and Rebellion: Slave Resistance in Eighteenth Century Virginia*. New York: Oxford University Press, 1972.

137 Nash, Gary B., *Forging Freedom: The Formation of Philadelphia's Black Community, 1760–1840*. Cambridge, MA: Harvard University Press, 1988.

138 Nash, Gary B., *Race and Revolution*. Madison, WI: Madison House, 1990.

139 Nash, Gary B., *Red, White, and Black: The Peoples of Early America* (4th edn). New York: Prentice-Hall, 1999.

140 Oates, Stephen B., *The Fires of the Jubilee: Nat Turner's Fierce Rebellion*. New York: Harper and Row, 1975.

141 Oates, Stephen B., *To Purge this Land with Blood: A Biography of John Brown* (2nd edn). Amherst, MA: University of Massachusetts Press, 1984.

142 Oliver, Roland, *The African Experience: Major Themes in African History from Earliest Times to the Present*. New York: HarperCollins, 1991.

143 Painter, Nell Irvin, *Sojourner Truth: A Life, A Symbol*. New York: Norton, 1996.

144 Pease, Jane H. and William H. Pease, *They Who Would Be Free: Blacks' Search for Freedom, 1830–1861*. New York: Athenaeum, 1974.

145 Perry, Lewis, *Radical Abolitionism: Anarchy and the Government of God in Antislavery Thought*. Ithaca, NY: Cornell University Press, 1973.

146 Perry, Lewis and Michael Fellman, eds, *Antislavery Reconsidered: New Perspectives on the Abolitionists*. Baton Rouge, LA: University of Louisiana Press, 1979.

147 Pressly, Thomas J., *Americans Interpret Their Civil War* (2nd edn). New York: Free Press, 1965, pp. 291–328.

148 Quarles, Benjamin, *The Negro in the American Revolution*. 1961; reprint, New York: Norton, 1973.

149 Quarles, Benjamin, *Black Abolitionists*. 1969; reprint, New York: Oxford University Press, 1977.

150 Quarles, Benjamin, *Allies for Freedom: Blacks and John Brown*. New York: Oxford University Press, 1970.

151 Quist, John W., *Restless Visionaries: The Social Roots of Antebellum Reform in Alabama and Michigan*. Baton Rouge, LA: Louisiana State University Press, 1998.

152   Rawley, James, *Race and Politics: 'Bleeding Kansas' and the Coming of the Civil War*. Philadelphia, PA: Lippincott, 1969.

153   Rayback, Joseph G., *Free Soil: The Election of 1848*. Lexington, KY: University Press of Kentucky, 1970.

154   Richards, Leonard L., *'Gentlemen of Property and Standing': Anti-Abolitionist Mobs in Jacksonian America*. New York: Oxford University Press, 1970.

155   Richards, Leonard L., *The Life and Times of Congressman John Quincy Adams*. Oxford University Press, 1991.

156   Roediger, David, *The Wages of Whiteness: Race and the Making of the American Working Class*. New York: Verso, 1991.

157   Rose, Willie Lee, *Rehearsal for Reconstruction: The Port Royal Experiment*. New York: Oxford University Press, 1964.

158   Rossbach, Jeffery S., *Ambivalent Conspirators: John Brown, the Secret Six, and a Theory of Slave Violence*. Philadelphia, PA: University of Pennsylvania Press, 1982.

159   Runyon, Randolph Paul, *Delia Webster and the Underground Railroad*. Lexington, KY: University Press of Kentucky, 1996.

160   Sanchez-Eppler, Karen, *Touching Liberty: Abolitionism, Feminism, and the Politics of the Body*. Berkeley, CA: University of California Press, 1993.

161   Schor, Joel, *Henry Highland Garnet: A Voice of Black Radicalism in the Nineteenth Century*. Westport, CT: Greenwood, 1977.

162   Schroeder, John H., *Mr. Polk's War: American Opposition and Dissent, 1846–1848*. Madison, WI: Madison House, 1971.

163   Sears, Richard, *A Utopian Experiment in Kentucky: Integration and Social Equality at Berea, 1866–1904*. Westport, CT: Greenwood, 1996.

164   Sellers, Charles G., *The Market Revolution: Jacksonian America, 1815–1846*. New York: Oxford University Press, 1991.

165   Sewell, Richard H., *John P. Hale and the Politics of Abolition*. Cambridge, MA: Harvard University Press, 1965.

166   Sewell, Richard H., *Ballots for Freedom: Antislavery Politics in the United States, 1837–1860*. New York: Oxford University Press, 1976.

167   Slaughter, Thomas, *Bloody Dawn: The Christiana Riot and Racial Violence in the Antebellum North*. New York: Oxford University Press, 1991.

168   Soderlund, Jean R., *Quakers and Slavery: A Divided Spirit*. Princeton, NJ: Princeton University Press, 1985.

169   Stampp, Kenneth M., *The Peculiar Institution: Slavery in the Antebellum South*. 1956; reprint, New York: Vintage Books, 1989.

170   Stanton, William R., *The Leopard's Spots: Scientific Attitudes toward Race in America, 1815–1859*. Chicago, IL: University of Chicago Press, 1960.

171   Staudenraus, Philip J., *The African Colonization Movement*. New York: Columbia University Press, 1961.

172   Sterling, Dorothy, *Ahead of Her Time: Abby Kelley and the Politics of Antislavery*. New York: Norton, 1992.

173   Stewart, James Brewer, *Joshua R. Giddings and the Tactics of Radical Politics*. Cleveland, OH: Case-Western Reserve University Press, 1970.

174   Stewart, James Brewer, *Wendell Phillips, Liberty's Hero*. Baton Rouge, LA: Louisiana State University Press, 1986.

175 Stewart, James Brewer, *William Lloyd Garrison and the Challenge of Emancipation*. Arlington Heights, IL: Harlan Davidson, 1992.

176 Stewart, James Brewer, *Holy Warriors: The Abolitionists and American Slavery* (revised edn). New York: Hill and Wang, 1997.

177 Thomas, John L., *The Liberator, William Lloyd Garrison: A Biography*. Boston, MA: Little, Brown, 1963.

178 Thomas, Lamont D., *Rise To Be a People: A Biography of Paul Cuffe*. Urbana, IL: University of Illinois Press, 1986.

179 Tise, Larry E., *Proslavery: A History of the Defense of Slavery in America, 1701–1840*. Athens, GA: University of Georgia Press, 1987.

180 Tyson, John S., *Elisha Tyson, the Philanthropist*. Baltimore, MD: B. Lundy, 1825.

181 US Congress. House. *Special Report of the Commissioner of Education*. House Exec. Doc. 315, 41 Cong., 2 sess. Serial 1427 (1870).

182 Van Deusen, Glyndon, *William Henry Seward*. New York: Oxford University Press, 1967.

183 Venet, Wendy Hammand, *Neither Ballots Nor Bullets: Women Abolitionists and Emancipation during the Civil War*. Charlottesville, VA: University of Virginia Press, 1991.

184 Volpe, Vernon L., *Forlorn Hope of Freedom: The Liberty Party in the Old Northwest, 1838–1848*. Kent, OH: Kent State University Press, 1990.

185 Walters, Ronald G., *The Antislavery Appeal: American Abolitionism after 1830*. Baltimore, MD: Johns Hopkins University Press, 1976.

186 Walters, Ronald G., *American Reformers, 1815–1860*. New York: Hill and Wang, 1978.

187 Wiecek, William W., *The Sources of Antislavery Constitutionalism in America*. Ithaca, NY: Cornell University Press, 1977.

188 Wilson, Carol, *Freedom at Risk: The Kidnapping of Free Blacks in America, 1780–1865*. Lexington, KY: University Press of Kentucky, 1995.

189 Wilson, Ellen Gibson, *The Loyal Blacks*. New York: G.P. Putnam's Sons, 1976.

190 Wright, Donald R., *African Americans in the Early Republic, 1789–1831*. Arlington Heights, IL: Harland Davidson, 1993.

191 Wyatt-Brown, Bertram, *Lewis Tappan and the Evangelical War against Slavery*. Cleveland, OH: Case-Western Reserve University Press, 1969.

192 Wyatt-Brown, Bertram, *Southern Honor: Ethics and Behavior in the Old South*. New York: Oxford University Press, 1982.

193 Wyatt-Brown, Bertram, *Yankee Saints and Southern Sinners*. Baton Rouge, LA: Louisiana State University Press, 1985.

194 Yacavone, Donald, *Samuel Joseph May and the Dilemmas of the Liberal Persuasion, 1797–1871*. Philadelphia, PA: Temple University Press, 1991.

195 Yee, Shirley J., *Black Women Abolitionists: A Study in Activism, 1828–1860*. Knoxville, TN: University of Tennessee Press, 1992.

196 Yellin, Jean Fagan, *Women and Sisters: The Antislavery Feminists and American Culture*. New Haven, CT: Yale University Press, 1990.

197 Yellin, Jean Fagan and John Van Horn, eds, *The Abolitionist Sisterhood: Women's Political Cultures in Antebellum America*. Ithaca, NY: Cornell University Press, 1994.

198   Zilversmit, Arthur, *The First Emancipation: The Abolition of Slavery in the North*. Chicago, IL: University of Chicago Press, 1967.

SECONDARY SOURCES: ARTICLES

199   Abzug, Robert H., 'The Influence of Garrisonian Abolitionists' Fear of Slave Violence on the Antislavery Argument', *Journal of Negro History* 55 (January 1970): 15–28.
200   Aptheker, Herbert, 'The Negro in the Abolitionist Movement', *Science and Society* 5 (Winter 1941): 2–23.
201   Clark, Elizabeth B., '"The Sacred Rights of the Weak": Pain, Sympathy, and the Culture of Individual Rights in Antebellum America', *Journal of American History* 82 (September 1995): 463–93.
202   Curry, Richard O., 'The Abolitionists and Reconstruction: A Critical Appraisal,' *Journal of Southern History* 34 (November 1968): 527–45.
203   Demos, John, 'The Anti-Slavery Movement and the Problem of Violent Means', *New England Quarterly* 37 (December 1964): 501–26.
204   Dew, Charles B., 'Black Ironworkers and the Slave Insurrection Panic of 1856', *Journal of Southern History* 61 (August 1975): 321–38.
205   Dillon, Merton L., 'The Abolitionists: A Decade of Historiography, 1959–1969', *Journal of Southern History* 35 (November 1969): 500–22.
206   Dixon, Christopher, 'A True Manly Life: Abolitionism and the Masculine Ideal', *Mid-America* 77 (Fall 1995): 213–36.
207   Finnie, Gordon E., 'The Antislavery Movement in the Upper South before 1840', *Journal of Southern History* 35 (August 1969): 319–42.
208   Fladeland, Betty, 'Who Were the Abolitionists?', *Journal of Negro History* 49 (April 1964): 81–115.
209   Fladeland, Betty, 'Revisionists vs. Abolitionists: The Historiographical Cold War of the 1930s and 1940s', *Journal of the Early Republic* 6 (Spring 1986): 1–21.
210   Friedman, Lawrence J., '"Historical Topics Sometimes Run Dry": The State of Abolitionist Studies', *Historian* 43 (February 1981): 177–94.
211   Gara, Larry, 'Slavery and the Slave Power: A Crucial Distinction', *Civil War History* 15 (March 1969): 5–18.
212   Gara, Larry, 'A Glorious Time: The 1874 Abolitionist Reunion in Chicago', *Journal of Illinois Historical Society* 65 (Autumn 1972): 280–92.
213   Harrold, Stanley, 'The Intersectional Relationship between Cassius M. Clay and the Garrisonian Abolitionists', *Civil War History* 35 (June 1989): 101–19.
214   Harrold, Stanley, ' 'Violence and Nonviolence in Kentucky Abolitionism', *Journal of Southern History* 57 (February 1991): 15–38.
215   Harrold, Stanley, 'Freeing the Weems Family: A New Look at the Underground Railroad', *Civil War History* 42 (December 1996): 289–306.
216   Harrold, Stanley, 'On the Borders of Slavery and Race: Charles T. Torrey and the Underground Railroad', *Journal of the Early Republic* 20 (Summer 2000): 273–9.
217   Hoganson, Kristan, 'Garrisonian Abolitionists and the Rhetoric of Gender, 1850–1860', *American Quarterly* 45 (December 1993): 558–95.

218   Huston, James L., 'The Experiential Basis of the Northern Antislavery Impulse', *Journal of Southern History* 56 (November 1990): 192–215.

219   Huston, James L., 'Property Rights in Slavery and the Coming of the Civil War', *Journal of Southern History* 65 (May 1999): 249–86.

220   Johnson, Clifton H., 'Abolitionist Missionary Activities in North Carolina', *North Carolina Historical Review* 40 (July 1963): 295–320.

221   Litwack, Leon, 'The Emancipation of the Negro Abolitionist', in Martin Duberman, ed., *The Antislavery Vanguard*. Princeton, NJ: Princeton University Press, 1965, pp. 137–55.

222   Loveland, Ann C., 'Evangelicalism and Immediate Emancipation in American Antislavery Thought,' *Journal of Southern History* 32 (May 1966): 172–88.

223   McKivigan, John R., 'The Antislavery Comeouter Sects: An Overlooked Abolitionist Strategy', *Civil War History* 26 (June 1980): 142–61.

224   McKivigan, John R., 'The Frederick Douglass–Gerrit Smith Friendship and Political Abolitionism in the 1850s', in Eric J. Sundquist, ed., *Frederick Douglass: New Literary and Historical Essays*. New York: Cambridge University Press, 1996, pp. 205–37.

225   Pease, Jane H. and William H. Pease, 'Confrontation and Abolition in the 1850s', *Journal of American History* 58 (March 1972): 923–37.

226   Pease, Jane H. and William H. Pease, 'Ends, Means, and Attitudes: Black-White Conflict in the Antislavery Movement', *Civil War History* 18 (June 1972): 117–28.

227   Pierson, Michael D., 'Between Antislavery and Abolition: The Politics of Jane Grey Swisshelm', *Pennsylvania History* 53   (Summer 1991): 693–710.

228   Rotundo, E. Anthony, 'Learning about Manhood: Gender Ideals and the Middle-class Family in Nineteenth-century America', in J.A. Mangan and James Welvin, eds, *Manliness and Morality: Middle-Class Masculinity in Britain and America, 1800–1940*. New York: Manchester University Press, 1987.

229   Stewart, James Brewer, 'The Aims and Impact of Garrisonian Abolitionism, 1840–1860', *Civil War History* 15 (September 1969): 197–209.

230   Stewart, James Brewer, 'Peaceful Hopes and Violent Experiences: The Evolution of Radical and Reforming Abolitionism, 1831–1837', *Civil War History* 17 (December 1971): 293–309.

231   Stewart, James Brewer, 'Young Turks and Old Turkeys: Abolitionists, Historians, and Aging Processes', *Reviews in American History* 11 (June 1983): 226–32.

232   Stewart, James Brewer. 'The Emergence of Racial Modernity and the Rise of the White North', *Journal of the Early Republic* 18 (Spring 1998): 181–217.

233   Stuckey, Stirling, 'A Last Stern Struggle: Henry Highland Garnet and Liberation Theory', in Leon Litwack and August Meier, eds, *Black Leaders of the Nineteenth Century*. Urbana, IL: University of Illinois Press, 1988, pp. 129–47.

234   Takaki, Ronald, 'The Black Child-Savage in Antebellum America', in Gary B. Nash and Richard Weiss, eds, *The Great Fear: Race in the Mind of America*. New York: Rinehart and Winston, 1970, pp. 27–44.

235   Thompson, Priscilla, 'Harriet Tubman, Thomas Garrett, and the Underground Railroad', *Delaware History* 22 (September 1986): 1–21.

236 Volpe, Vernon L., 'The Liberty Party and Polk's Election, 1844', *Historian* 53 (Summer 1991): 693–710.

237 Wyatt-Brown, Bertram, 'The Abolitionists' Postal Campaign of 1835', *Journal of Negro History* 50 (October 1965): 227–38.

238 Wyatt-Brown, Bertram, 'The Abolitionist Controversy: Men of Blood, Men of God', in Howard H. Quint and Milton Cantor, eds, *Men, Women, and Issues in American History* (2 vols). Homewood, IL: Dorsey, 1980. Vol. 1, pp. 230–48.

INDEX

SEMINAR STUDIES IN HISTORY

General Editors: Clive Emsley & Gordon Martel

The series was founded by Patrick Richardson in 1966. Between 1980 and 1996 Roger Lockyer edited the series before handing over to Clive Emsley (Professor of History at the Open University) and Gordon Martel (Professor of International History at the University of Northern British Columbia, Canada and Senior Research Fellow at De Montfort University).

MEDIEVAL ENGLAND

The Pre-Reformation Church in England 1400–1530 (Second edition)
Christopher Harper-Bill   0 582 28989 0

Lancastrians and Yorkists: The Wars of the Roses
David R Cook   0 582 35384 X

TUDOR ENGLAND

Henry VII (Third edition)
Roger Lockyer & Andrew Thrush   0 582 20912 9

Henry VIII (Second edition)
M D Palmer   0 582 35437 4

Tudor Rebellions (Fourth edition)
Anthony Fletcher & Diarmaid MacCulloch   0 582 28990 4

The Reign of Mary I (Second edition)
Robert Tittler   0 582 06107 5

Early Tudor Parliaments 1485–1558
Michael A R Graves   0 582 03497 3

The English Reformation 1530–1570
W J Sheils   0 582 35398 X

Elizabethan Parliaments 1559–1601 (Second edition)
Michael A R Graves   0 582 29196 8

England and Europe 1485–1603 (Second edition)
Susan Doran   0 582 28991 2

The Church of England 1570–1640
Andrew Foster   0 582 35574 5

STUART BRITAIN

Social Change and Continuity: England 1550–1750 (Second edition)
Barry Coward   0 582 29442 8

James I (Second edition)
S J Houston   0 582 20911 0

The English Civil War 1640–1649
Martyn Bennett   0 582 35392 0

Charles I, 1625–1640
Brian Quintrell   0 582 00354 7

The English Republic 1649–1660 (Second edition)
Toby Barnard   0 582 08003 7

Radical Puritans in England 1550–1660
R J Acheson   0 582 35515 X

The Restoration and the England of Charles II (Second edition)
John Miller   0 582 29223 9

The Glorious Revolution (Second edition)
John Miller   0 582 29222 0

EARLY MODERN EUROPE

The Renaissance (Second edition)
Alison Brown   0 582 30781 3

The Emperor Charles V
Martyn Rady   0 582 35475 7

French Renaissance Monarchy: Francis I and Henry II (Second edition)
Robert Knecht   0 582 28707 3

The Protestant Reformation in Europe
Andrew Johnston   0 582 07020 1

The French Wars of Religion 1559–1598 (Second edition)
Robert Knecht   0 582 28533 X

Phillip II
Geoffrey Woodward   0 582 07232 8

The Thirty Years' War
Peter Limm   0 582 35373 4

Louis XIV
Peter Campbell   0 582 01770 X

Spain in the Seventeenth Century
Graham Darby   0 582 07234 4

Peter the Great
William Marshall   0 582 00355 5

EUROPE 1789–1918

Britain and the French Revolution
Clive Emsley — 0 582 36961 4

Revolution and Terror in France 1789–1795 (Second edition)
D G Wright — 0 582 00379 2

Napoleon and Europe
D G Wright — 0 582 35457 9

Nineteenth-Century Russia: Opposition to Autocracy
Derek Offord — 0 582 35767 5

The Constitutional Monarchy in France 1814–48
Pamela Pilbeam — 0 582 31210 8

The 1848 Revolutions (Second edition)
Peter Jones — 0 582 06106 7

The Italian Risorgimento
M Clark — 0 582 00353 9

Bismarck & Germany 1862–1890 (Second edition)
D G Williamson — 0 582 29321 9

Imperial Germany 1890–1918
Ian Porter, Ian Armour and Roger Lockyer — 0 582 03496 5

The Dissolution of the Austro-Hungarian Empire 1867–1918 (Second edition)
John W Mason — 0 582 29466 5

Second Empire and Commune: France 1848–1871 (Second edition)
William H C Smith — 0 582 28705 7

France 1870–1914 (Second edition)
Robert Gildea — 0 582 29221 2

The Scramble for Africa (Second edition)
M E Chamberlain — 0 582 36881 2

Late Imperial Russia 1890–1917
John F Hutchinson — 0 582 32721 0

The First World War
Stuart Robson — 0 582 31556 5

EUROPE SINCE 1918

The Russian Revolution (Second edition)
Anthony Wood — 0 582 35559 1

Lenin's Revolution: Russia, 1917–1921
David Marples — 0 582 31917 X

Stalin and Stalinism (Second edition)
Martin McCauley — 0 582 27658 6

The Weimar Republic (Second edition)
John Hiden   0 582 28706 5

The Inter-War Crisis 1919–1939
Richard Overy   0 582 35379 3

Fascism and the Right in Europe, 1919–1945
Martin Blinkhorn   0 582 07021 X

Spain's Civil War (Second edition)
Harry Browne   0 582 28988 2

The Third Reich (Second edition)
D G Williamson   0 582 20914 5

The Origins of the Second World War (Second edition)
R J Overy   0 582 29085 6

The Second World War in Europe
Paul MacKenzie   0 582 32692 3

Anti-Semitism before the Holocaust
Albert S Lindemann   0 582 36964 9

The Holocaust: The Third Reich and the Jews
David Engel   0 582 32720 2

Britain and Europe since 1945
Alex May   0 582 30778 3

Eastern Europe 1945–1969: From Stalinism to Stagnation
Ben Fowkes   0 582 32693 1

The Khrushchev Era, 1953–1964
Martin McCauley   0 582 27776 0

NINETEENTH-CENTURY BRITAIN

Britain before the Reform Acts: Politics and Society 1815–1832
Eric J Evans   0 582 00265 6

Parliamentary Reform in Britain c. 1770–1918
Eric J Evans   0 582 29467 3

Democracy and Reform 1815–1885
D G Wright   0 582 31400 3

Poverty and Poor Law Reform in Nineteenth-Century Britain, 1834–1914:
From Chadwick to Booth
David Englander   0 582 31554 9

The Birth of Industrial Britain: Economic Change, 1750–1850
Kenneth Morgan   0 582 29833 4

Chartism (Third edition)
Edward Royle   0 582 29080 5

Peel and the Conservative Party 1830–1850
Paul Adelman   0 582 35557 5

Gladstone, Disraeli and later Victorian Politics (Third edition)
Paul Adelman   0 582 29322 7

Britain and Ireland: From Home Rule to Independence
Jeremy Smith   0 582 30193 9

TWENTIETH-CENTURY BRITAIN

The Rise of the Labour Party 1880–1945 (Third edition)
Paul Adelman   0 582 29210 7

The Conservative Party and British Politics 1902–1951
Stuart Ball   0 582 08002 9

The Decline of the Liberal Party 1910–1931 (Second edition)
Paul Adelman   0 582 27733 7

The British Women's Suffrage Campaign 1866–1928
Harold L Smith   0 582 29811 3

War & Society in Britain 1899–1948
Rex Pope   0 582 03531 7

The British Economy since 1914: A Study in Decline?
Rex Pope   0 582 30194 7

Unemployment in Britain between the Wars
Stephen Constantine   0 582 35232 0

The Attlee Governments 1945–1951
Kevin Jefferys   0 582 06105 9

The Conservative Governments 1951–1964
Andrew Boxer   0 582 20913 7

Britain under Thatcher
Anthony Seldon and Daniel Collings   0 582 31714 2

INTERNATIONAL HISTORY

The Eastern Question 1774–1923 (Second edition)
A L Macfie   0 582 29195 X

The Origins of the First World War (Second edition)
Gordon Martel   0 582 28697 2

The United States and the First World War
Jennifer D Keene   0 582 35620 2

Anti-Semitism before the Holocaust
Albert S Lindemann   0 582 36964 9

The Origins of the Cold War, 1941–1949 (Second edition)
Martin McCauley   0 582 27659 4

Russia, America and the Cold War, 1949–1991
Martin McCauley   0 582 27936 4

The Arab–Israeli Conflict
Kirsten E Schulze   0 582 31646 4

The United Nations since 1945: Peacekeeping and the Cold War
Norrie MacQueen   0 582 35673 3

Decolonisation: The British Experience since 1945
Nicholas J White   0 582 29087 2

The Vietnam War
Mitchell Hall   0 582 32859 4

WORLD HISTORY

China in Transformation 1900–1949
Colin Mackerras   0 582 31209 4

US HISTORY

America in the Progressive Era, 1890–1914
Lewis L Gould   0 582 35671 7

The United States and the First World War
Jennifer D Keene   0 582 35620 2

The Truman Years, 1945–1953
Mark S Byrnes   0 582 32904 3

The Vietnam War
Mitchell Hall   0 582 32859 4

American Abolitionists
Stanley Harrold   0 582 35738 1

The American Civil War, 1861–1865
Reid Mitchell   0 582 31973 0